How to access your on-line resources

Kaplan Financial students will have a MyKaplan account and these extra resources will be available to you online. You do not need to register again, as this process was completed when you enrolled. If you are having problems accessing online materials, please ask your course administrator.

If you are not studying with Kaplan and did not purchase your book via a Kaplan website, to unlock your extra online resources please go to www.en-gage.co.uk (even if you have set up an account and registered books previously). You will then need to enter the ISBN number (on the title page and back cover) and the unique pass key number contained in the scratch panel below to gain access.

You will also be required to enter additional information during this process to set up or confirm your account details.

If you purchased through the Kaplan Publishing website you will automatically receive an e-mail invitation to register your details and gain access to your content. If you do not receive the e-mail or book content, please contact Kaplan Publishing.

Your code and information

This code can only be used once for the registration of one book online. This registration and your online content will expire when the final sittings for the examinations covered by this book have taken place. Please allow one hour from the time you submit your book details for us to process your request.

Please scratch the film to access your unique code.

Please be aware that this code is case-sensitive and you will need to include the dashes within the passcode, but not when entering the ISBN.

Operational Level

Subject E1

Managing Finance in a Digital World

EXAM PRACTICE KIT

British Library Cataloguing-in-Publication Data

A catalogue record for this book is available from the British Library.

Published by:

Kaplan Publishing UK
Unit 2 The Business Centre
Molly Millar's Lane
Wokingham
Berkshire
RG41 2QZ

ISBN: 978-1-78740-720-6

© Kaplan Financial Limited, 2020

Kaplan Publishing's learning materials are designed to help students succeed in their examinations. In certain circumstances, CIMA can make post-exam adjustment to a student's mark or grade to reflect adverse circumstances which may have disadvantaged a student's ability to take an exam or demonstrate their normal level of attainment (see CIMA's Special Consideration policy). However, it should be noted that students will not be eligible for special consideration by CIMA if preparation for or performance in a CIMA exam is affected by any failure by their tuition provider to prepare them properly for the exam for any reason including, but not limited to, staff shortages, building work or a lack of facilities etc.

Similarly, CIMA will not accept applications for special consideration on any of the following grounds:

- failure by a tuition provider to cover the whole syllabus

- failure by the student to cover the whole syllabus, for instance as a result of joining a course part way through

- failure by the student to prepare adequately for the exam, or to use the correct pre-seen material

- errors in the Kaplan Official Study Text, including sample (practice) questions or any other Kaplan content or

- errors in any other study materials (from any other tuition provider or publisher).

CONTENTS

	Page
Index to questions and answers	P.5
Exam techniques	P.7
Syllabus guidance, learning objectives and verbs	P.9
Approach to revision	P.13
Syllabus grids	P.15

Section

1	Objective test questions	1
2	Answers to objective test questions	53

Quality and accuracy are of the utmost importance to us so if you spot an error in any of our products, please send an email to mykaplanreporting@kaplan.com with full details.

Our Quality Co-ordinator will work with our technical team to verify the error and take action to ensure it is corrected in future editions.

INDEX TO QUESTIONS AND ANSWERS

OBJECTIVE TEST QUESTIONS

EXAM TECHNIQUES

COMPUTER-BASED ASSESSMENT

Golden rules

1   Make sure you have completed the compulsory 15-minute tutorial before you start the test. This tutorial is available through the CIMA website and focusses on the functionality of the exam. You cannot speak to the invigilator once you have started.

2   These exam practice kits give you plenty of exam style questions to practise so make sure you use them to fully prepare.

3   Attempt all questions, there is no negative marking.

4   Double check your answer before you put in the final answer although you can change your response as many times as you like.

5   Not all questions will be multiple choice questions (MCQs) – you may have to fill in missing words or figures.

6   Identify the easy questions first and get some points on the board to build up your confidence.

7   Attempt 'wordy' questions first as these may be quicker than the computation style questions. This will relieve some of the time pressure you will be under during the exam.

8   If you don't know the answer, flag the question and attempt it later. In your final review before the end of the exam try a process of elimination.

9   Work out your answer on the whiteboard provided first if it is easier for you. There is also an onscreen 'scratch pad' on which you can make notes. You are not allowed to take pens, pencils, rulers, pencil cases, phones, paper or notes into the testing room.

SYLLABUS GUIDANCE, LEARNING OBJECTIVES AND VERBS

A CIMA 2019 PROFESSIONAL QUALIFICATION

Details regarding the content of the CIMA 2019 professional qualification can be located within the CIMA 2019 professional qualification syllabus document.

You can use the following diagram showing the whole structure of your qualification to help you keep track of your progress. Make sure you seek appropriate advice if you are unsure about your progression through the qualification.

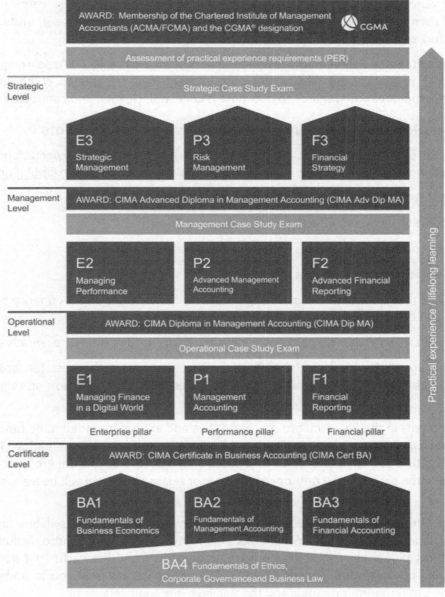

Reproduced with permission from CIMA

B   STUDY WEIGHTINGS

Each Objective Test comprises 60 questions drawn from across individual subjects of the syllabus in line with the weightings for each content area as set out in the blueprint.

C   LEARNING OUTCOMES

Each subject within the qualification is divided into a number of broad syllabus topics. The topics contain one or more lead learning outcomes, related component learning outcomes and indicative knowledge content.

A learning outcome has two main purposes:

1   to define the skill or ability that a well-prepared candidate should be able to exhibit in the examination

2   to demonstrate the approach likely to be taken by examiners in examination questions.

The learning outcomes are part of a hierarchy of learning objectives. The verbs used at the beginning of each learning outcome relate to a specific learning objective, e.g. understand how data is collected, cleaned and connected by finance.

The verb 'understand' indicates a low-level learning objective (level 1/2). As learning objectives are hierarchical, it is expected that at this level students will be able to comprehend ideas, concepts and techniques with regards to how data is collected, cleaned and connected by finance.

The examination blueprints and representative task statements

CIMA have also published examination blueprints giving learners clear expectations regarding what is expected of them. This can be accessed here www.cimaglobal.com/examblueprints

The blueprint is structured as follows:

- Exam content sections (reflecting the syllabus document)

- Lead and component outcomes (reflecting the syllabus document)

- Representative task statements.

A representative task statement is a plain English description of what a CIMA finance professional should know and be able to do.

The content and skill level determine the language and verbs used in the representative task.

CIMA will test up to the level of the task statement in the objective test (an objective test question on a particular topic could be set at a lower level than the task statement in the blueprint).

The task statements in the blueprint are representative and are not intended to be (nor should they be viewed as) an all-inclusive list of tasks that may be tested on the Examination. It also should be noted that the number of tasks associated with a particular content group or topic is not indicative of the extent such content group, topic or related skill level will be assessed on the test.

The format of the objective test blueprints follows that of the published syllabus for the 2019 CIMA Professional Qualification. Weightings for content sections are also included in the individual subject blueprints. A list of the learning objectives and the verbs that appear in the syllabus learning outcomes and examinations follows and these will help you to understand the depth and breadth required for a topic and the skill level the topic relates to.

CIMA verb hierarchy

Skill level	Verbs used	Definition
Level 5 Evaluation How you are expected to use your learning to evaluate, make decisions or recommendations	Advise	Counsel, inform or notify
	Assess	Evaluate or estimate the nature, ability or quality of
	Evaluate	Appraise or assess the value of
	Recommend	Propose a course of action
	Review	Assess and evaluate in order, to change if necessary
Level 4 Analysis How you are expected to analyse the detail of what you have learned	Align	Arrange in an orderly way
	Analyse	Examine in detail the structure of
	Communicate	Share or exchange information
	Compare and contrast	Show the similarities and/or differences between
	Develop	Grow and expand a concept
	Discuss	Examine in detail by argument
	Examine	Inspect thoroughly
	Interpret	Translate into intelligible or familiar terms
	Monitor	Observe and check the progress of
	Prioritise	Place in order of priority or sequence for action
	Produce	Create or bring into existence
Level 3 Application How you are expected to apply your knowledge	Apply	Put to practical use
	Calculate	Ascertain or reckon mathematically
	Conduct	Organise and carry out
	Demonstrate	Prove with certainty or exhibit by practical means
	Prepare	Make or get ready for use
	Reconcile	Make or prove consistent/compatible
Level 2 Comprehension What you are expected to understand	Describe	Communicate the key features of
	Distinguish	Highlight the differences between
	Explain	Make clear or intelligible/state the meaning or purpose of
	Identify	Recognise, establish or select after consideration
	Illustrate	Use an example to describe or explain something
Level 1 Knowledge What you are expected to know	List	Make a list of
	State	Express, fully or clearly, the details/facts of
	Define	Give the exact meaning of
	Outline	Give a summary of

D OBJECTIVE TEST

Objective test

Objective test questions require you to choose or provide a response to a question whose correct answer is predetermined.

The most common types of objective test question you will see are:

- Multiple choice, where you have to choose the correct answer(s) from a list of possible answers. This could either be numbers or text.

- Multiple response, for example, choosing two correct answers from a list of eight possible answers. This could either be numbers or text.

- Fill in the blank (numerical answers only), where you fill in your answer within the provided space.

- Drag and drop, for example, matching a technical term with the correct definition.

- Hot spots, where you select an answer by clicking on graphs/diagrams.

Guidance re CIMA on-screen calculator

As part of the CIMA objective test software, candidates are now provided with a calculator. This calculator is on-screen and is available for the duration of the assessment. The calculator is available in each of the objective tests and is accessed by clicking the calculator button in the top left hand corner of the screen at any time during the assessment. Candidates are permitted to utilise personal calculators as long as they are an approved CIMA model. CIMA approved model list is found here: https://www.cimaglobal.com/Studying/study-and-resources/.

All candidates must complete a 15-minute exam tutorial before the assessment begins and will have the opportunity to familiarise themselves with the calculator and practise using it. The exam tutorial is also available online via the CIMA website. Candidates can use their own calculators providing it is included in CIMA's authorised calculator listing.

Fundamentals of objective tests

The objective tests are 90-minute assessments comprising 60 compulsory questions, with one or more parts. There will be no choice and all questions should be attempted. All elements of a question must be answered correctly for the question to be marked correctly. All questions are equally weighted.

APPROACH TO REVISION

Stage 1: Assess areas of strengths and weaknesses

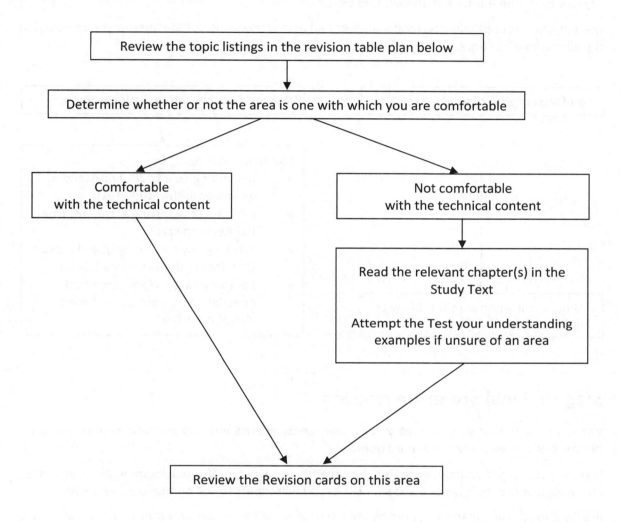

Stage 2: Question practice

Follow the order of revision of topics as recommended in the revision table plan below and attempt the questions in the order suggested.

Try to avoid referring to text books and notes and the model answer until you have completed your attempt.

Try to answer the question in the allotted time.

Review your attempt with the model answer and assess how much of the answer you achieved in the allocated exam time.

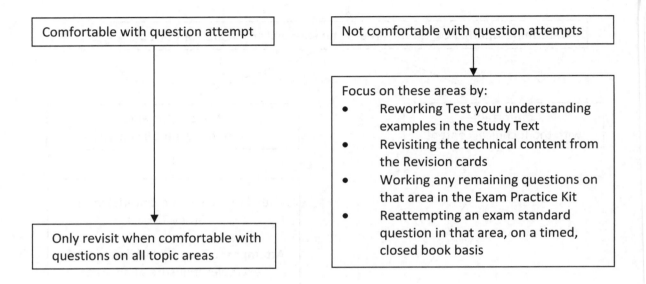

Stage 3: Final pre-exam revision

We recommend that you **attempt at least one ninety minute mock examination** containing a set of previously unseen exam standard questions.

It is important that you get a feel for the breadth of coverage of a real exam without advanced knowledge of the topic areas covered – just as you will expect to see on the real exam day.

Ideally a mock examination offered by your tuition provider should be sat in timed, closed book, real exam conditions.

SYLLABUS GRIDS

E1: Managing Finance in a Digital World

How the finance function is organised

Content weighting

Content area		Weighting
A	Role of the Finance Function	20%
B	Technology in a Digital World	20%
C	Data and Information in a Digital World	20%
D	Shape and Structure of the Finance Function	20%
E	Finance Interacting with the Organisation	20%
		100%

E1A: Role of the Finance Function

This section examines the roles that finance plays in organisations and why. It describes in detail the activities that finance professionals perform to fulfil these roles. Consequently, it is the foundation of the whole qualification and answers the question: what do finance professionals do and why? It provides links with other topics within the subject and what is covered in other areas of the Operational Level.

Lead outcome	Component outcome	Topics to be covered	Explanatory notes
1. Explain the roles of the finance function in organisations.	Explain how the finance function: a. Enables organisations to create and preserve value b. Shapes how organisations create and preserve value c. Narrates how organisations create and preserve value	• The fast-changing and unpredictable contexts in which organisations operate • Enabling value creation through planning, forecasting and resource allocation • Shaping value creation through performance management and control • Narrating the value creation story through corporate reporting • The role of ethics in the role of the finance function	Describe the increasingly disruptive contexts in which organisations and their finance teams operate and how these contexts shape the role of finance. Take each role and show how finance performs it in a typical organisational setting. The coverage should be introductory and brief. It is meant to set the scene for subsequent sections and draw a link between the roles and the topics that will be covered in other areas of the Operational Level.
2. Describe the activities that finance professionals perform to fulfil the roles.	Describe how the finance function: a. Collates data to prepare information about organisations b. Provides insight to users by analysing information c. Communicates insight to influence users d. Supports the implementation of decisions to achieve the desired impact e. Connects the different activities connect to each other	• How data is collected, cleaned and connected by finance • Types of analysis to produce insights • How finance communicates to influence key stakeholders (audiences, frequency, format, etc.) • How finance uses resource allocation and performance management to enable organisations to achieve their objectives • Potential impact of technology	Use 'information to impact' framework to describe the primary activities finance professionals perform. Relate it to how data is generated, transformed and used. Link it to how technology could be used to improve the productivity of finance professionals in these areas and the threat of automation.

E1B: Technology in a Digital World

This section focuses on the technologies that define and drive the digital world in which finance operates. It provides awareness of the technologies used in organisations and deepens understanding of the impact of the technologies on what finance does. It draws on the issues raised in the previous section about the role of finance and the activities finance performs to fulfil these roles. Given that the digital world is underpinned by technology and the use of data, this section provides a foundation to the next section on data.

Lead outcome	Component outcome	Topics to be covered	Explanatory notes
1. Outline and explain the technologies that affect business and finance.	a. Outline the key features of the fourth industrial revolution. b. Outline and explain the key technologies that define and drive the digital world.	• Characteristics and dynamics of the fourth industrial revolution • Cloud computing • Big data analytics • Process automation • Artificial intelligence • Data visualisation • Blockchain • Internet of things • Mobile • 3-D printing	The aim is to create awareness of the technologies that drive the digital world and how they interact with each other. The technologies outlined by the major advisory firms and the World Economic Forum digital transformation initiative provide the material on which learning and related activities can be based.
2. Examine how the finance function uses digital technologies to fulfil its roles.	Examine how finance uses the following to guide how it performs its roles: a. Digital technology b. Digital mindsets c. Automation and the future of work d. Ethics of technology usage	• How finance uses technologies listed above • Areas of finance susceptible to automation and why • New areas for finance to focus on • Digital mindsets for finance • Ethics of the use of technology	Examine how finance professionals use the relevant technologies to fulfil their roles. Explain how the technologies affect various activities finance professionals perform in the 'information to impact' framework. The intention is to move from creating awareness to generating understanding of how finance can use these technologies to increase its value and relevance to organisations.

E1C: Data and Information in a Digital World

This section draws out one of the major implications of using technology in organisations and the finance function – namely the collection and processing of information can be done more effectively by machines rather than by people. It asserts that the role of finance professionals should be to use data to create and preserve value for organisations. Five ways of using data are examined. The key competencies required to use data in these ways are also highlighted. The primary objective is to help finance professionals understand what they can do with data and how to build the skills needed to use data.

Lead outcome	Component outcome	Topics to be covered	Explanatory notes
1. Describe the ways in which data is used by the finance function.	Identify the ways in which the finance function uses data: a. In a general sense b. Specifically in each of the primary activities of finance	Using data for: • Decision-making • Understanding the customer • Developing customer value proposition • Enhancing operational efficiency • Monetising data • Ethics of data usage	Build on the previous section on technology to explain why, in the digital world, finance professionals must place more focus on using information than on collecting and/or processing information. Outline and describe the various uses of information. Link them to the primary activities that the finance function performs and to the topics to be covered in other modules of the Operational Level.
2. Explain the competencies required to use data to create and preserve value for organisations.	Explain the competencies that finance professionals need in: a. Data strategy and planning b. Data engineering, extraction and mining c. Data modelling, manipulation and analysis d. Data and insight communication	• Assessment of data needs • Extraction, transformation and loading (ETL) systems • Business Intelligence (BI) systems • Big data analytics • Data visualisation	Highlight and explain the data competencies required in the digital world. Locate where finance has a competitive advantage and where finance will need to work with data scientists.

E1D: Shape and Structure of the Finance function

This section brings together the implications of the previous sections. It reveals how the finance function is structured and shaped. This structure and shape enables finance to perform its role in the organisation and with other internal and external stakeholders. In this sense, it prepares candidates for the next section, which looks at how finance interacts with key internal stakeholders in operations, marketing and human resources.

Lead outcome	Component outcome	Topics to be covered	Explanatory notes
1. Describe the structure and shape of the finance function.	Describe the: a. Evolution of the shape of the finance function b. Shape of the finance function in the digital era	• Structure of the finance function from the roles that generate information to the roles that turn information into insight and communicate insight to decision-makers • Hierarchical shape of finance function • Shared services and outsourcing of finance operations • Retained finance • Automation and diamond shape of finance function	Introduce candidates to the structure of the finance function and outline the broad areas of finance such as finance operations, external reporting, financial planning and analysis (FP&A), decision support etc. Describe the evolving shape of the finance function from the triangle to the diamond shape. Link the description to the impact of digital technology and automation on the finance function.
2. Explain what each level of the finance function does.	Explain the activities of: a. Finance operations b. Specialist areas including financial reporting and financial planning and analysis (FP&A) c. Strategic partnering for value d. Strategic leadership of the finance team	• Finance operations to generate information and preliminary insight • FP&A, taxation, corporate reporting, decision support to produce insight • Business partnering to influence organisation to make appropriate decisions • Leading the finance team to create the required impact for the organisation	The focus is the diamond shape and the four levels within this shape. Explain what each level does, the relationship between the levels, and the link between the levels and the basic finance activities covered under the role of finance.

E1E: Finance Interacting with the Organisation

The finance function is not the only area of activity in organisations. Finance joins with others to create and preserve value for their organisations. This section brings together what has been learned in the previous section to describe how finance can interact with other parts of the organisation to achieve the objectives of finance, those other areas and crucially the objectives of the whole organisation. The aim is to show how finance can work collaboratively in a connected (and joined-up) organisation and not in isolation.

Lead outcome	Component outcome	Topics to be covered	Explanatory notes
1. Describe how the finance function interacts with operations.	Describe: a. Main role of operations b. Areas of interface with finance c. Key performance indicators	• Process management • Product and service management • Supply chain management	Describe how finance plays its role by interacting with the rest of the organisation. Bring together the issues raised in the previous sections and link them to what the other areas of the organisations do. For example, address how finance and marketing interact using data and collaborative technology to achieve organisational goals and the individual functional goals of both finance and marketing. Describe how the use of KPIs influence these interactions and how the KPIs of finance and these areas can be aligned to ensure they work together effectively.
2. Describe how the finance function interacts with sales and marketing.	Describe: a. Main role of sales and marketing b. Areas of interface with finance c. Key performance indicators	• Market segmentation • Big data analytics in marketing • Channel management • Sales forecasting and management	
3. Describe how the finance function interacts with human resources.	Describe: a. Main role of human resources b. Areas of interface with finance c. Key performance indicators	• Staff acquisition • Staff development • Performance management • Motivation and reward systems	
4. Describe how the finance function interacts with IT.	Describe: a. Main role of IT b. Areas of interface with finance c. Key performance indicators	• IT infrastructure • IT systems support • Costs and benefits of IT systems	

Information concerning formulae and tables will be provided via the CIMA website: www.cimaglobal.com.

Section 1

OBJECTIVE TEST QUESTIONS

All the section objective questions carry the same number of marks.

SYLLABUS SECTION A: ROLE OF THE FINANCE FUNCTION

1 Stan is trying to work out how many staff members are going to be required to work on a project next week.

   Which role of the finance function best describes what Stan is doing?

   A   Resource allocation

   B   Performance management and control

   C   Planning

   D   Financial (corporate) reporting

2 JKP Company is reviewing its corporate governance procedures after the internal auditors raised the issue at the monthly meeting of major shareholders. TG, the chairperson and CEO of the company, feels that the company's current focus on its five-year strategic plan demonstrates that its corporate governance procedures are already working well.

   Which of the following issues at JKP suggest that there is poor corporate governance at the firm?

   A   Lack of independent scrutiny

   B   Lack of contact with shareholders

   C   Emphasis on short-term profitability

   D   Domination of the board

3 BJY Company is a FTSE 150 company and is governed by the UK corporate governance code. The remuneration committee is chaired by LK, the company chairman. LK, three non-executive directors (NEDs) and one executive director sit on the committee. All five have been on the committee for the past 15 months.

Which TWO of the following features of the committee put it in breach of the UK corporate governance code?

A   Company chairman sits on the committee

B   Company chairman chairs the committee

C   Only three NEDS sit on the committee

D   An executive director sits on the committee

E   The chair has only been on the committee for the previous 15 months

4   Match the following descriptions to the ethical principle they describe.

Completing work carefully, thoroughly and diligently, in accordance with relevant technical and professional standards.	Integrity
Being straightforward, honest and truthful in all professional and business relationships.	Confidentiality
Non-disclosure of information unless you have specific permission or a legal or professional duty to do so.	Professional behaviour
Not allowing bias, conflict of interest, or the influence of other people to override your professional judgement.	Professional competence and due care
Compliance with relevant laws and regulations.	Objectivity

5 Polly, a CIMA member in practice, has been asked to complete an important task. However, she is very pushed for time and knows she will not be able to complete it properly.

Which ethical principle is under threat?

A   Integrity

B   Confidentiality

C   Professional competence and due care

D   Professional behaviour

E   Objectivity

6 Gemma, a CIMA member in practice, has been told by her boss that there are going to be some redundancies in the company. She has been reassured that her job is safe but has been told of a number of colleagues whose jobs are at risk. One of these colleagues is a close friend of Gemma who she knows is about to buy a new house.

If Gemma warns her friend about the redundancy plans which ethical principle is most under threat?

A Integrity

B Confidentiality

C Professional competence and due care

D Professional behaviour

E Objectivity

7 Which THREE of the following are benefits of a company behaving in an ethical manner?

A Improve reputation

B Attract high calibre employees

C Increased costs

D Increased risk

E Increased sales

8 Which THREE of the following would be considered to be connected stakeholders?

A Employees

B Government

C Environmental pressure groups

D Suppliers

E Customers

F Lenders

9 The directors of ECC Ltd are proposing the introduction of many corporate social responsibility (CSR) initiatives. However, their shareholders are not convinced that it is worth the increased cost to the business.

Which THREE of the following are arguments for the introduction of CSR initiatives?

A Strengthens the brand

B Acts as a method of differentiation

C Increases costs

D Attracts new customers

E Is a public relations (PR) exercise

10   The risk that the directors may run the company in their own interests, rather than those of the shareholders is known as the agency problem.

Is this statement true or false?

11   **Which THREE the following symptoms can indicate that there is poor corporate governance?**

   A   Increasing contact with shareholders

   B   Domination of the board

   C   Lack of internal audit

   D   Emphasis on long-term profitability

   E   Lack of supervision of employees

12   **Which of the following statements is/are true?**

   (i)   In the UK, Corporate Governance is a principles based system.

   (ii)   In the US, Corporate Governance is a rules based system.

   A   Statement (i) only

   B   Statement (ii) only

   C   Neither of them

   D   Both of them

13   The finance function has three main roles; it 'enables', 'shapes how' and 'narrates how' value is created and preserved.

Which of the following would the finance function carry out to 'shape how' the organisation creates and preserves value?

   A   Performance management and control

   B   Planning and forecasting

   C   Financial (corporate) reporting

   D   Planning, forecasting and resource allocation

14   **Using the principles of good corporate governance, which THREE committees should a company make use of?**

   A   Nominations committee

   B   Remuneration committee

   C   Ethics committee

   D   Governance committee

   E   Board committee

   F   Audit committee

15   According to the UK Corporate Governance Code, a company can improve corporate governance by ensuring that:

A   The chairman and chief executive are the same individual in order to avoid confusion over who has responsibility for running the company.

B   The chairman and chief executive are different individuals in case one dies or becomes ill.

C   The company chairman is remunerated in line with the performance of the company.

D   The chairman and chief executive are different individuals in order to prevent one person having too much power within the company.

16   Kay is a senior employee of Henshaw plc and is considering becoming a NED after she retires.

After how many years will she be classified as an independent NED?

A   4 years

B   5 years

C   6 years

D   7 years

17   **Churchman plc is looking to appoint new members to its board of directors. Which committee should they consult before making such appointments?**

A   Appointments committee

B   Directors committee

C   Committee of NEDs

D   Nominations committee

18   **The argument that companies should operate solely to make money for shareholders and that it is not a company's role to worry about social responsibilities is the viewpoint of:**

A   Modernists

B   Everyone

C   Traditionalists

D   The government

19   **What are the three classifications of stakeholders commonly known as?**

A   Internal, external, connected

B   Shareholders, employees, customers

C   Internal, external, regulated

D   Connected, unconnected, external

20 Match the stakeholder with their need/expectation of the company.

Stakeholder	Need/expectation
Government	Pay, working conditions and job security
Shareholders	Dividends and capital growth
Employees	Provision of taxes and jobs and compliance with legislation
Customers	Value-for-money products and services

21 Which of the following statements is/are true?

(i)   The chairman is the person in charge of running the company.

(ii)   The chief economic officer is the person in charge of running the board.

A   Statement (i)

B   Statement (ii)

C   Both of them

D   Neither of them

22 Complete the following sentences by placing one of the following options in the spaces.

The preparation of forecasts, for example of future sales or material prices, will be an important role of the finance function _____ .

The preparation of comprehensive reports for shareholders will be an important role of the finance function _____ .

The preparation of variance analysis for control purposes will be an important role of the finance function _____ .

Options:
in narrating how the organisation creates and preserves value
in enabling the organisation to create and preserve value
in shaping how the organisation creates and preserves value

23 Which of the following organisations is normally found in the public sector?

A   Schools

B   Charities

C   Clubs

D   Businesses

24   **Which of the following statements is/are true?**

(i)   The finance function will help shape how an organisation creates and preserves value through financial (corporate reporting).

(ii)   The finance function merely records what has happened over the period in question and as long as it can do that it shouldn't need to be proactive in the way that it is organised.

A   Statement (i)

B   Statement (ii)

C   Both of them

D   Neither of them

25   Which of the following is an example of poor corporate social responsibility?

A   The sacking of an employee for gross misconduct

B   Building a product with a known failure rate

C   The advertising of cigarettes on early evening TV

D   A significant redundancy programme

26   What is the generally accepted definition of agency risk?

A   The risk that agency staff are less experienced than fulltime employees and hence are more likely to make mistakes.

B   The risk that government agencies will interfere with the company's procedures resulting in excessive costs.

C   Directors, as agents of the owners will act in a way that is contrary to the wishes of those owners.

D   Employees, as agents to the directors will act in a way that is contrary to the wishes of those directors.

27   Changes brought about by technology are greatly changing the shape of the finance function. However, not-for-profit organisations will not be affected as their primary objective is not a profit motive.

Is this statement true or false?

28   Which of the following TWO statements are true with regards to change in the modern world?

A   Change always increases the risks faced by an organisation

B   Change is so unpredictable that there is no point in having long-term plans

C   A key driver of change in the modern world is the rapid advancements in technology

D   Changing customers' expectations cannot be ignored if a business wants to remain competitive

E   Change does not affect really small enterprises

29 Jemima has been asked to collect some information for her manager. It takes her 14 hours to gather the information and when she presents it to her manager it is immediately filed away.

Which of the characteristics of good quality information is not being exhibited?

A   Understandable

B   Complete

C   Cost < benefit

D   Accurate

30 **Which of the following is NOT one of the 5 As of a finance professional's basic activities?**

A   Assemble

B   Apply

C   Acumen

D   Advise

E   Align

31 **Which of the 5 As of a finance professional's basic activities includes collecting data from a variety of sources?**

A   Acumen

B   Advise

C   Assemble

D   Adapt

E   Accumulate

32 Data consists of raw fact and figures, whilst information is data that has been processed?

Is this statement true or false?

33 **Which of the 5 As of a finance professional's basic activities includes comparing actual information to budgeted information?**

A   Assemble

B   Analyse

C   Advise

D   Apply

E   Acumen

34 **Which THREE of the following may be limitations of using external data sources?**

A   It may be out of date

B   It may be more difficult to gather

C   It has no relevance to the organisation using it

D   It may not be accurate

E   It is unethical to use someone else's data

35 **Which type of information cannot normally be expressed in numerical terms?**

A   Quantitative

B   Qualitative

C   Financial

D   Non-financial

37 **Which THREE of the following are examples of internal sources of data?**

A   Purchase ledger data

B   Payroll data

C   Newspaper articles

D   Exchange rate data

E   Production data

37 **At what stage within the information to impact framework is the finance function most predominantly focussed on guidance and management?**

A   Information

B   Insight

C   Influence

D   Impact

38 David is examining a report that has been prepared by a junior member of the finance team. He has noticed there are a lot of spelling mistakes and not all of the figures add up.

Which of the characteristics of "good" information is not being exhibited?

A   Accurate

B   Complete

C   Understandable

D   Relevant

39 Eliza is currently in the process of comparing budgeted sales data to actual data and trying to investigate reasons for the variances.

Using the information to impact framework, which stage would best describe Eliza's current activity?

A   Information

B   Insight

C   Influence

D   Impact

40 **Which of the following statements regarding the analysis of quantitative data is correct?**

A   Sales growth of 20% year on year represents significant growth.

B   Non-financial data cannot be quantified and therefore has less analysis value than financial data.

C   Good quality analysis relies upon a representative sample of the population.

D   Number of training days taken per employee is not an example of quantitative data.

41 **During which stage of the information to impact framework are solutions typically deployed?**

A   Information

B   Insight

C   Influence

D   Impact

42 Performance measures can be both qualitative and quantitative.

Which THREE of the following would be classified as quantitative performance measures?

A   Customer satisfaction rating

B   Sales

C   Level of innovation

D   Staff productivity

E   Profit

F   Units produced

43 **Which of the following roles performed by the accounting function at LPW Company would be best described as 'Impact' in the 'Information to Impact' framework'?**

A   Setting market prices to improve market share

B   Compiling reports on current pricing structures

C   Forecasting likely sales figures based on market conditions

D   Monitoring compliance with industry regulations

44   VJ, the management accountant at GDH Company has been reviewing the outcome of the current product development strategy. VJ's aim is to understand how the decision-making process at GDH, including its use of key data, could be improved in future.

Which of the following finance activities does this represent?

A   Acumen

B   Assembling information

C   Advising to influence

D   Analysing for insights

E   Profit

F   Units produced

SYLLABUS SECTION B: TECHNOLOGY IN A DIGITAL WORLD

45   **"A rapid and major change in an economy, driven by a shift in the methods and types of work undertaken" best describes what?**

A   Globalisation

B   An industrial revolution

C   The digital age

D   Political instability

46   **How is the delivery of on-demand computing resources otherwise known?**

A   Artificial Intelligence

B   The Internet of things

C   Big data

D   Cloud computing

47   **The process by which users log on to remote servers to access and process their files is best known as what?**

A   Cloud computing

B   Wide Area Network

C   The internet

D   Remote working

48   **What are the TWO main types of cloud computing?**

A   Public Cloud

B   Restricted Cloud

C   Private Cloud

D   Amazon Cloud

49 **Which THREE of the following are disadvantages of cloud computing?**

  A Scalability

  B Contract management

  C Potential job losses

  D Reliance on a third party

  E Increases cost

  F Reduced flexibility for employees

50 **Which THREE of the following statements relating to big data are true?**

  A Big data refers to any financial data over $1 billion

  B The defining characteristics of big data are velocity, volume and variety

  C Managing big data effectively can lead to increased competitive advantage

  D The term big data means 'data that comes from many sources'

  E Big data contains both financial and non-financial data

51 **How might the following sources of data be classified?**

  Select from the following: Human Sourced, Machine Generated, Processed, Open

  A National Statistics

  B Social media posts

  C Emails

  D Smart meters

  E Customer database

  F Census

  G Home assistants

  H Fixed asset register

52 **Which of the following sentences is true?**

  A Process automation is only feasible for simple, repetitive tasks

  B Process automation in complex business areas is beyond the limits of technology

  C Process automation can enable a business to save costs

  D Process automation usually leads to employee dissatisfaction

53 **Machines working and reacting like human beings describes what?**

  A Robotics

  B Voice recognition

  C Artificial intelligence

  D The 4th Industrial Revolution

54   **Which of the following is a definition of a blockchain?**

A   A technology that allows people who do not know each other to trust a shared record of events.

B   A centralised, undistributed and private digital ledger that is used to record transactions.

C   A sequence of transactions facilitated by the internet.

D   A supply chain management system used to improve efficiency.

55   **Which THREE of the following statements about a blockchain are true?**

A   Blockchain is regarded as a solution to cyber security risk

B   Records in the blockchain are publically available and distributed across everyone that is part of the network of participants

C   Records in the blockchain are always kept private to enhance security

D   The verification of transactions is carried out by computers

E   The verification of transaction is carried out by individuals

56   **What is the internet of things?**

A   An interactive collection of websites enabling users to communicate with one another.

B   A technology that allows people who do not know each other to trust a shared record of event.

C   Smart phones that enable users to control appliances within their home such as their heating or lighting.

D   A network of smart devices with inbuilt software and connectivity which connect to the internet.

57   Advancements in mobile technology have contributed to the decline in the newspaper industry?

Is this statement true or false?

58   CDMA is the technology that has transformed mobile technology.

What does CDMA stand for?

A   Coded data mobile application

B   Code-division multiple access

C   Cloud data mobile access

D   Computer device mobile acceleration

59 How is "additive manufacturing", creating a product layer by layer, better known?

    A   Cellular manufacturing

    B   Lean manufacturing

    C   3-D printing

    D   Blockchain technology

60 Which THREE of the following are consequences of the developments in mobile technologies?

    A   The decline of the newspaper industry

    B   The decline of social media interactions

    C   The decline in the number of retail bank branches

    D   An increase in the on demand nature of music

    E   An increase in the cost to manufacture smart devices

61 Which THREE of the following are advantages of 3-D printing?

    A   Gaining economies of scale through the ability to batch produce

    B   Increased throughput speed from design to print

    C   Off-cuts can be recycled into future products

    D   Maintenance of Intellectual Property

    E   Customisation of design leading to competitive advantage

62 Which THREE of the following are advantages of cloud computing?

    A   Cost efficiency

    B   Scalability

    C   Flexibility

    D   Contract management

    E   Career opportunities

    F   Highlights inefficiencies

63 Assessing the reliability of big data refers to which of the 4 Vs?

    A   Velocity

    B   Volume

    C   Visibility

    D   Veracity

64   **Which of the following statements about data visualisation is true?**

A   The most common use of data visualisation is the creation of a dashboard displaying real time KPIs.

B   Data is always displayed in standardised formats to ensure consistency.

C   Data visualisation refers to data that is analysed using virtual reality software.

D   Increased use of data visualisation within organisations increases the need for more IT experts.

65   TPO Company manufactures jewellery and has been looking at ways to improve its customers' experience. It has decided to enable customers to customise their purchases. The company's first goal is to identify the preferences of its different customer groups.

Which of the following tools will help TPO achieve this goal?

A   Artificial intelligence

B   Data analytics

C   Process automation

D   Data visualisation

66   GHP Company manufactures chilled meals for resale to supermarkets. As part of GHP's recent technological upgrade, and as part of its adoption of the benefits of the internet of things, the company has installed a new temperature control for the mechanical cooling system in the warehouse where the meals are stored.

Which THREE of the following features of the control are possible because of the internet of things?

A   Sensing the current temperature inside the warehouse and adjusting the output of the mechanical cooling system accordingly

B   Responding to remote instructions from the company's head office to alter the temperature in the warehouse

C   Tracking the anticipated external temperature and pre-emptively adjusting the internal temperature in the warehouse

D   Gathering and feeding back temperature and cooling systems data to GHP

E   Controlling the temperature to within 0.05 degrees to ensure adherence to national food storage regulations.

67   **Technologies which are anticipated to update existing systems to improve capability are often referred to as what?**

A   Core modernisation tools

B   Exponentials

C   Innovators

D   The digital age

68 Technologies which will deliver new capabilities are often referred to as what?

A   Core modernisation tools

B   Exponentials

C   Innovators

D   The digital age

69 Which of the following is a disadvantage of cloud computing?

A   Increased flexibility to working arrangements

B   More reliance on third party suppliers

C   Access to continually up to date software

D   Easier integration of systems

70 Cloud computing enables multiple users to collaborate on a file at the same time, although this increases the risk of version control issues.

Is this statement true or false?

A   True

B   False

71 Which THREE of the following are advantages of investing in process automation within the finance function?

A   Staff time can be freed up to focus on value adding activities

B   No extra training will be required for staff as they will no longer be processing manually

C   Staff will automatically buy in to having the mundane work taken from them

D   Headcount reductions

E   Improved efficiency

72 The provision of information in a more appealing and understandable manner is often referred to as what?

A   Artificial Intelligence

B   Data simplification

C   Cloud computing

D   Data visualisation

73 Which of the following is not necessarily a benefit of data visualisation?

A   Improves the accuracy of the data being analysed

B   Problem areas can be identified sooner

C   Understandable by many users

D   Supports prompt decision making

74   **Which of the following statements regarding blockchain are true?**

(i)   Blockchain technology involves the use of a distributed ledger.

(ii)   Cryptocurrencies should be considered as intangible assets in the financial statements.

(iii) The use of blockchain technologies removes the need for traditional intermediaries in transactions.

(iv)   Blockchain solutions will not overcome the issue of slow cross border payments.

A   (i) and (ii)

B   (i) and (iii)

C   (iii) and (iv)

D   (i), (ii) and (iii)

75   **How has 3-D printing primarily impacted the finance function?**

A   Impacted the costings of operations

B   Facilitated the creation of assets

C   Driven higher revenues

D   Increased inventories

76   **Which THREE of the following are qualities identified by Forbes as being important dimensions of the digital mind set?**

A   Provide vision yet empower others

B   Have the imagination to innovate

C   Be sceptical yet open minded

D   Sustain yet disrupt

E   Retain control yet be open minded

77   Book-my-room is a broker facilitating the letting of private accommodation between individuals.

Which of the following is a likely consequence for their financial statements?

A   Their network of contracts will be recognised as an intangible asset on their statement of financial position.

B   The true value of Book-my-room may be understated on their statement of financial position.

C   The expenses on the statement of profit or loss will be overstated.

D   Their statement of cashflows will be reduced as the private individuals sort payment of the lettings out between themselves.

78 **Which of the following statements about big data and the internal audit function are true?**

    A   The emergence of big data has improved the accuracy of data which means smaller sample sizes now need to be tested.

    B   Internal audit will now be testing and analysing larger populations of data.

    C   Big data has no relevance to the internal audit function.

    D   Big data will contribute to the development of more efficient and insightful management control systems and budgeting processes.

79 Cryptocurrencies should be accounted for as cash and cash equivalents on the statement of financial position?

Is this statement true or false?

    A   True

    B   False

80 So Handy is a relatively young business comprising a franchised network of labourers such as plumbers, electricians and carpenters. Each franchisee has an app that enables them to log and record the expenses they incur as well as scanning all receipts for materials purchased.

What type of technology are they making use of?

    A   Social media

    B   Internet of things

    C   An intranet

    D   Mobile technology

81 Technological developments are driving an increase in process automation. Consequently, some of the traditional skills of a finance professional such as data collection and processing will need to be replaced with higher-level skills.

Which skill is required to make decisions and evaluate data sources?

    A   Analytical skills

    B   People skills

    C   Judgement

    D   Leadership

82 During her appraisal interview, Edie's line manager praises her for having a good understanding of the business environment.

Which essential skill is Edie displaying?

    A   Business acumen

    B   Leadership skills

    C   Judgement

    D   Analytical skills

83   **Which THREE of the following are principles within GDPR?**

    A   Data must not be kept for longer than five years

    B   Data must be used for a specified, explicit purpose

    C   Data held must be accurate

    D   Data must be used transparently

    E   Data should always be in a hard copy format

84   Compliance with GDPR is the only thing that matters where data usage is concerned.

    Is this statement true or false?

    A   True

    B   False

85   Corporate digital responsibility (CDR) involves a commitment to protect customers.

    Which TWO of the following statements are true about CDR?

    A   It demonstrates an awareness of the risks associated with data

    B   It is unnecessary as all data regulations are covered within GDPR

    C   It is a voluntary commitment to go beyond mere compliance with legislation

    D   It is a legal requirement for any organisation that holds data about its customers

86   **In the context of CDR, which of the following is an example of "digital inclusion"?**

    A   Incentivising customers to give more data

    B   The customer's ability to opt in and be rewarded for sharing data

    C   Helping and supporting customers to access the online digital world

    D   A bank using a customer's financial information to help them improve their financial management

87   **What is meant by digital inclusion?**

    A   The use of technology to analyse an entire data population rather than a sample

    B   The need to reward and incentivise customers to provide companies with data

    C   The attempt to ensure that all members of society have the skills and tools to access the online digital world

    D   The use of blockchain technology to synchronise data and transactions across a network

88   **Which THREE of the following are important dimensions of a digital mindset?**

    A   Empowering employees to take action to adapt the organisation

    B   Letting go of existing business practices in favour of new ideas

    C   Fully embracing and exploring new technologies

    D   Trusting intuition and vision to focus on change

    E   Maintaining a clear vision of how the business should change

SYLLABUS SECTION C: DATA AND INFORMATION IN A DIGITAL WORLD

89   **Match each of the below individuals to the level of decision-making they are involved in.**

   Pick from the following options: Strategic, Tactical and Operational

   Jane is reviewing the staffing rota for the coming week to see if extra staff are needed.

   Bill is a director of the company currently involved in an acquisition decision.

   Colleen is choosing which products will be stocked in each of the stores around the country.

90   Providing insightful information to the organisation can enhance the competitive advantage, however, will also always increase the costs to the business.

   Is this statement true or false?

   A   True

   B   False

91   **Which THREE of the following are ways that data and technology can support the marketing function?**

   A   Comparing prices with competitors

   B   Assessing the viability of market segments

   C   Improving efficiencies in the supply chain

   D   Preventative maintenance of products

   E   Personalising communications with customers

92   **Which THREE of the following are ways that data and technology can support operations?**

   A   Identifying bottlenecks in processes

   B   Preventative maintenance of products

   C   Forecasting production

   D   Identifying training needs of employees

   E   Targeting customers with offers

93   **Images, audio files and animations are all examples of what?**

   A   Technology

   B   Big data

   C   Information

   D   Digital assets

OBJECTIVE TEST QUESTIONS : SECTION 1

94 Taylor Training Co produced a bank of educational videos that students can access at any time to support their learning.

These videos are examples of what for Taylor Training Co?

A   Tangible non-current asset

B   Digital asset

C   Video asset

D   Customer asset

95 **Which TWO of the following are features of a DAMS?**

A   Decentralised digital asset access

B   Open access to any user

C   Facilitated by cloud based software

D   Single central location for digital asset storage

96 Because digital assets are stored on the cloud it makes them less secure than if they were stored on a hard drive.

Is this statement true or false?

A   True

B   False

97 **How are medium-term decisions better known?**

A   Strategic

B   Managerial

C   Operational

D   Tactical

98 **What does the acronym DAMS stand for?**

A   Data and marketing strategy

B   Digitised automatic management system

C   Digital asset management system

D   Data assisted management strategy

99 There are three levels of decision making; strategic, tactical and operational.

In this context which of the following statements are true?

(i)   Strategic decisions are clearly important but without good tactical support, good strategic decisions may never be realised.

(ii) Operational decision-making may be the last of the three but poor operational decisions will often cause costs to spiral out of control.

A   (i) only

B   (ii) only

C   Both are true

D   Neither are true

100 Which of the following would be correctly described as information to the sales director of a business?

A   The invoice total of a sale made

B   The average daily sales per department

C   The lead time expected on raw materials

D   The sales price list for the company products

101 'The process of safeguarding important information from corruption, compromise or loss' is the definition of what?

A   Corporate social responsibility

B   GDPR

C   Corporate digital responsibility

D   Data protection

102 In the context of data gathering and quality, which of the following statements are true?

(i)   The technology available merely takes the legwork out of data gathering, everything that is available now was available in the past, but it was too time consuming to gather it.

(ii) With the improved data comes with it the need to be able to respond quickly. Shorter lead times are an essential aspect of improved data.

A   (i) only

B   (ii) only

C   Both are true

D   Neither are true

103 In the context of digital asset management systems (DAMS) which of the following statements are true?

(i) Once someone has permission to use (say) an image there is nothing to stop them sharing that image with others.

(ii) Once someone has permission to use (say) an image then there is nothing to stop them using that image for longer than it was intended.

A (i) only

B (ii) only

C Both are true

D Neither are true

104 Which of the following best describes tactical decision-making?

A Long-term decisions made by senior management

B Decisions made repeatedly over the short term

C Decisions which impact the entire organisation

D Decisions involving putting the strategic plan into action

105 Beth and her colleagues at the same level of the organisational hierarchy are in discussions about which, if any, acquisitions to make using the surplus funds of the business. They are choosing between two similar businesses.

Which level of decision-making are they engaging in?

A Strategic

B Tactical

C Acquisitional

D Operational

106 Maypole ltd has been analysing various aspects of the data that it collects. Their data analyst has identified that parents with children of a particular age are regularly searching for products on their website.

Which benefit of data analytics is specifically being exhibited?

A Enhanced data transparency

B Efficiency gains

C Enhanced performance

D Market customisation

107 Data which gives insight into the relationship between a product launch and subsequent sales helps with which one aspect of the marketing mix?

    A   Product

    B   Price

    C   Place

    D   Promotion

108 Connecting machines on the internet of things to collect real time data has many advantages for a manufacturing business.

Monitoring the performance of the machines enables which of the following advantages specifically?

    A   Forecasting

    B   Preventative maintenance

    C   Improved service for customers

    D   Supply chain collaboration

109 In the context of GDPR, which of the following statements are true?

    (i)   The storage of data is not covered by the legislation, it is more about how the data is used.

    (ii)   The data that is allowed to be stored is basically the same for all business.

    A   (i) only

    B   (ii) only

    C   Both are true

    D   Neither are true

110 Which stakeholder of the finance function is most likely to require data on competitors' pricing strategies?

    A   Sales

    B   Production

    C   Shareholders

    D   Employees

111 Which stakeholder of the finance function is most likely to require data on employee productivity?

    A   Production

    B   Employees

    C   HR

    D   Shareholders

112 **Which stakeholder of the finance function is most likely to require data on market trends?**

A   Employees

B   Sales

C   Production

D   Shareholders

113 Directors will be the stakeholder of the finance function most likely to require data visualisation.

Is this statement true or false?

A   True

B   False

114 **What are the three stages in transferring data? (in the correct order)**

A   Loading, extraction, transformation

B   Input, process, output

C   Extraction, transformation, loading

D   Extraction, converting, warehousing

115 A data model considers the data of an organisation in a systematic way that allows it to be stored and retrieved in an efficient and effective manner.

Match the level of data modelling with its description

Level	Description
Conceptual	This level begins to develop a technical map of rules and data structures defining how data will be held and used
Logical	This considers how the defined system requirements will be implemented using a specific database management system
Physical	Business oriented and practical, considering the business data and its requirements

116 **What can be described as "a coherent approach for organising, governing, analysing and deploying an organisations information assets"**

A   Digital assets

B   Data strategy

C   Business Intelligence

D   Data warehousing

117   What does "the process of changing data to make it easier to read" describe?

A   Data mining

B   Data manipulation

C   Data modelling

D   Data query

118   Which of the 4 Vs of big data refers to the constant stream of data being produced?

A   Variety

B   Veracity

C   Volume

D   Velocity

119   What does "the technology driven process of analysing business data" describe?

A   Business intelligence

B   Big data

C   Data strategy

D   Data visualisation

120   Which of the following best describes an ETL system?

A   The process of harvesting data from source locations

B   The transformation of data into a suitable format

C   The uploading of clan data into a data warehouse

D   A single tool to automatically bring data sources into a destination system

121   The use of a dashboard to present data is an example of what?

A   Data visualisation

B   Data simplification

C   Graphical data

D   Information processing

122   The need for systems to validate data links to which of the 4 Vs of big data?

A   Variety

B   Veracity

C   Volume

D   Velocity

123 Technological advancements are constantly changing the skills and knowledge an organisation requires in a finance professional.

Which of the following skills will require the finance professional to build empathy and interactions with stakeholders?

A   Digital scientist skills

B   Leadership skills

C   Technical skills

D   People skills

124 **Interest cover, market value of non-current assets and the amount of existing loans are all types of data of most interest to:**

A   Shareholders

B   Directors

C   Employees

D   Lenders

125 **In relation to data, which of the following statements are true?**

(i)   One cannot have too much data, so an organisation should gather as much as possible.

(ii)   As far as sales prices are concerned a sales director just needs the average sales price achieved in the most recent reporting period to manage the business.

A   (i) only

B   (ii) only

C   Both are true

D   Neither are true

126 **An effective data strategy should consist of five elements; identify, store, provision, process and which other?**

A   Responsibility

B   Manage

C   Govern

D   Congruence

127 **Which of the following is not a level in a data modelling process?**

A   Physical

B   Structural

C   Conceptual

D   Logical

128 In the context of an ETL system, which of the following statements are true?

(i) Data is extracted and then profiled before being loaded in to the data warehouse.

(ii) Once data is profiled it is transformed to a suitable form before being extracted and loaded in to the data warehouse.

A   (i) only

B   (ii) only

C   Both are true

D   Neither are true

129 ELC Co has produced some infographics to enable the visualisation of its sales data.

Which THREE of the following characteristics will make the infographics more effective?

A   Details of sales made to each customer on a daily basis

B   The ability to drill down to obtain further detail

C   Avoidance of technical jargon

D   Access granted to all sales staff

E   Intuitive visualisations needing little explanation

130 In the world of big data and the role of accountants, which of the following statements are true?

(i) Although there is more data, the basic analysis techniques used should be the same and so no upskilling is needed.

(ii) Experts may be needed to provide additional analysis of the data.

A   (i) only

B   (ii) only

C   Both are true

D   Neither are true

SYLLABUS SECTION D: SHAPE AND STRUCTURE OF THE FINANCE FUNCTION

131 HGD Company provides architectural drawings for use by construction companies and only employs architects that hold a qualification from the National Institute of Architects. Clients are charged by the hour for the architects' time.

Based on Mintzberg's 'effective organisation' framework which of the following coordinating mechanisms is most likely to be in place at HGD Company?

   A   Standardisation of work

   B   Standardisation of output

   C   Standardisation of skills

   D   Mutual adjustment

132 JJC Company is undergoing a restructuring process. No new staff are being recruited but three new managerial levels are being created and reporting lines are being redrawn to reflect the new roles.

Which THREE of the following changes would be expected as a result of this restructuring exercise?

   A   Increase in the scalar chain

   B   Widening of spans of control

   C   Greater chances of career progression

   D   Reduction in bureaucracy

   E   Increase in height of the organisation structure

133 **Which of the following statements regarding the entrepreneurial structure is correct?**

   A   It usually allows for defined career paths for employees

   B   It often enjoys strong goal congruence throughout the organisation

   C   It can normally cope with significant diversification and growth

   D   Control within the organisation tends to be weak

134 **Which of the following is a disadvantage of a functional structure?**

   A   Lack of economies of scale

   B   Absence of standardisation

   C   Specialists feel comfortable

   D   Empire building

135 **Which of the following is a characteristic of a matrix structure?**

A   Built around the owner manager, who makes all the decisions.

B   Appropriate for small companies which have few products and locations and which exist in a relatively stable environment.

C   Structured in accordance with product lines or divisions or departments.

D   Requires dual reporting to managers, for example when a project team member has to report to a project manager as well as a head of his functional department.

136 The following are attributes of either divisional or functional structures.

Which TWO of the following are features of the divisional structure?

A   Economies of scale are encouraged

B   Encourages standardisation of outputs and processes

C   Adaptable if further diversification is pursued

D   Senior managers are able to focus on strategic issues

137 H Co makes a variety of unrelated products, including bicycles, furniture and electronics. It is aware that each of these products requires very different strategies and functions. H wishes to use a structure that will allow for each product to be managed separately, but wishes to minimise its overall administrative costs.

Which of the following organisational structures would be most appropriate for H Co to adopt?

A   Divisional

B   Entrepreneurial

C   Functional

D   Matrix

138 **Which of the following structures results in a potential loss of control over key operating decisions and a reduction in goal congruence?**

A   Matrix

B   Entrepreneurial

C   Functional

D   Geographic

139 **In relation to organisational structures which of the following is the correct definition of the phrase 'span of control'?**

A   The number of employees that a manager is directly responsible for

B   The number of management levels in an organisational structure

C   The number of levels in the hierarchy below a given manager

D   The number of managers in the organisation

140   Correctly label the diagram using the options below

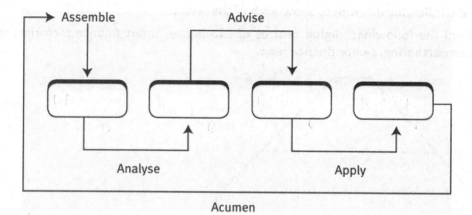

A   Impact

B   Insight

C   Influence

D   Information

141   Which of the finance functions basic activities has the greatest emphasis on accounting and governance rather than guidance and management?

A   Assemble

B   Analyse

C   Advise

D   Apply

142   Complete the following sentence to explain the development of the contemporary finance function.

Pick from the following words: innovation, assembly, advising, technology, analysis, automation, applying/execution

_____ and_____ will play an important role in all of the activities of the finance function but will have the largest impact on the _____ and_____ activities.

This will 'free up' the resource of the finance function professionals who can now place greater focus on the_____ and _____activities.

143 The shape of the finance function is changing into a diamond shape with four levels.

Label the following diagram to show each of the levels.

Pick from the following: digital centres of excellence, smart finance factories, strategic business partnering, senior finance team

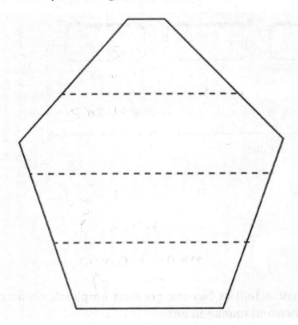

144 **Which of the following statements about outsourcing is/are correct?**

Statement	True?
An advantage of outsourcing is reduced headcount and therefore reduced cost.	
Outsourcing can enable an organisation to access expertise that it might otherwise be lacking.	
A drawback of outsourcing is that it distracts management and they lose focus on their core activities.	
Transaction costs are a benefit to the business.	
Outsourcing may lead to redundancies which can affect employee morale.	

145 **Which THREE of the following are advantages of setting up a shared service centre for the finance function?**

    A   Systems consolidation

    B   Increased control

    C   Empire building

    D   Consistency of reporting

    E   Advancements in technology

    F   It makes it easier to deal with cultural or language differences

146 **Transaction costs are expenses resulting from which of the following?**

    A   Outsourcing of services

    B   Offshoring of organisational functions

    C   Penetration pricing

    D   Organisational downsizing

147 **Complete the sentence below by placing one of the following options in the space.**

One of the main activities of the finance function is 'advising to influence'. Broadly speaking this can be referred to as _____ .

REPORTING	DEPLOYING SOLUTIONS	QUESTIONING	DEVELOPING SOLUTIONS

148 **Complete the sentence below by placing one of the following options in the space.**

A software-based approach that replicates user actions to reduce or eliminate human intervention in mundane, repetitive and manually intensive processes is called:

BPR	KAIZEN	TQM	RPA

149 **Which level of the finance function is more likely to focus on information for external stakeholders?**

    A   Operational

    B   Management

    C   Strategic

    D   External

150 Harry works in a large organisation which has both suppliers and customers all over the world. Harry is a CIMA qualified accountant and is responsible for managing foreign currency. In particular, Harry tries to minimise the company's exposure to foreign exchange losses.

What is Harry's role?

    A   Treasurer

    B   Management accountant

    C   Financial accountant

    D   Internal audit

151 **With regards to the management accounting function, which of the following statements is correct?**

    A   It is often used by external stakeholders, such as shareholders

    B   It is a requirement for all limited companies

    C   It is mainly a historic record of the organisation's activities

    D   It aids planning and decision making within the business

152 K Co has recently split its accounting function into two parts – one that deals with management accounting and the other with financial accounting.

    A   Management accounting

    B   Financial accounting

Match the following statements to either A (management accounting) or B (financial accounting).

    (i)   Preparation of the statement of profit or loss

    (ii)   Recording of business transactions

    (iii)   Preparation of statements for K Ltd's internal use

    (iv)   No legal formats used

153 The P/E ratio measures the profit attributable to each ordinary shareholder.

Is this statement true or false?

    A   True

    B   False

154 Which of the following functions is most likely to be undertaken in a treasury department?

    A   Preparation of cash flow statements

    B   Foreign currency management

    C   Product pricing decisions

    D   Key factor analysis

155 Which of the following is an important advantage of using loans to finance investment?

    A   Loan interest payments can usually be suspended if profits are low

    B   The timing of loan payments is often at the company's discretion

    C   Loan interest is tax deductible

    D   Banks will often not require security for loan advances

156 Company G is considering raising finance to invest in new premises. It believes that it should raise debt finance (rather than equity finance) by way of a bank loan.

Which of the following statements is correct regarding debt and equity finance?

    A   Debt tends to be cheaper to service than equity

    B   Interest payments can be suspended in the future if H is unable to afford them

    C   Dividends are an allowable deduction against H's profits

    D   H will likely need to provide asset security to investors whether it chooses to raise debt or equity finance

157 S decided to record the purchases made on the 2nd of April 200X in tax year ending 31st of March 200X. The authorities will likely classify this as tax _____.

Which of the following words correctly fill this gap?

A   Evasion

B   Minimisation

C   Avoidance

D   Suppression

158 **Tax mitigation involves which of the following?**

A   Taking all legal steps to reduce one's tax liability

B   Agreeing to pay a financial penalty to avoid prosecution

C   Moving businesses and funds offshore to reduce liability to UK tax

D   Reducing tax liabilities without frustrating the law makers' intentions

159 Below are a number of statements regarding internal and external audit.

Which FOUR of the statements relate to internal audit rather than external audit?

A   It is a legal requirement for larger companies

B   The scope of work is decided by management

C   Can be undertaken by employees of the company

D   Ultimately reports to the company's shareholders

E   Reviews whether financial statements are true and fair

F   Must be undertaken by independent auditors

G   Mainly focuses on reviewing internal controls

H   Ultimately reports to management

160 **What is the key purpose of internal audit?**

A   To detect errors and fraud

B   To evaluate the organisation's risk management processes and systems of control

C   To give confidence as to the truth and fairness of the financial statements

D   To express an internal opinion on the truth and fairness of the financial statements

161 **Which of the following specialist roles produce budgets to support the major decisions of the board?**

A   Financial Planning and Analysis

B   Taxation

C   Project Management

D   Project Appraisal

162 **Which of the following specialist roles focuses on an assessment and evaluation of the many decisions and potential outcomes of an investment decision.**

  A   Financial Planning and Analysis

  B   Taxation

  C   Project Management

  D   Project Appraisal

163 **Which of the following specialist roles integrate all aspects of a project?**

  A   Financial Planning and Analysis

  B   Taxation

  C   Project Management

  D   Project Appraisal

164 **Which of the following specialist roles includes providing information on capital investment decisions?**

  A   Financial Planning and Analysis

  B   Taxation

  C   Project Management

  D   Project Appraisal

165 **Are the following statements true or false?**

  A   Because of the ethical principle of confidentiality, specialists within the organisation cannot work with the finance function.

  B   Taxation specialists have a number of key responsibilities including the calculation and interpretation of key financial ratios.

  C   Projects can vary in size, resource allocation and complexity.

  D   When calculating a payback period today is known as time 0.

166 **Which THREE of the following explain recent changes to the specialist areas of an organisation?**

  A   There are now more opportunities for business partnering between the finance function and the specialist areas.

  B   The finance function is no longer a requirement because of advancements in technology.

  C   The shape of the finance function is now evolving to a diamond shape.

  D   The finance function is constantly improving the shared understanding of how an organisation creates value.

  E   "Digital centres of excellence" are now performing the routine management reporting tasks.

167 **Complete the following sentence by choosing from the options below.**

Level two of the diamond shaped finance function involves _____ insight to _____ users. This must be delivered in an appropriate _____ and with appropriate _____.

Influence	Communicating	Frequency	Marketing	Assertiveness	Format

168 **Working with internal and external stakeholders to influence how the organisation creates and preserves value is known as what?**

A   Business process re-engineering

B   Outsourcing the finance function

C   Strategic business partnering

D   Smart finance factories

169 **Which of the following statements about leadership of the finance team is/are correct?**

Statement	True/False?
The CEO is the leader of the finance team.	False
The leader of the finance team is responsible for executing and funding strategies.	True
The CFO needs a skill set outside of the traditional finance skills.	True
Technology has had minimal impact on the leader of the finance function as he/she is so senior in the organisation.	False

170 **Which TWO stages in the "information to impact" framework have been most affected by technology and automation?**

A   Analyse

B   Apply/execute

C   Assemble

D   Advise

171 Label the following diagram to match the finance activities to the structure of the modern finance function.

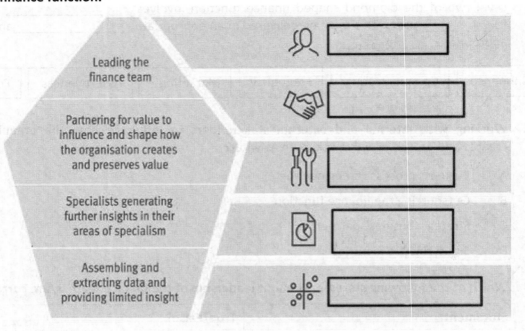

Use the following labels

- Data processing
- Managing others
- Stakeholder Interactions
- Data collection
- Applying expertise

172 Artificial intelligence (AI), machine learning and natural language programming are all examples of what?

A   Robotic Process Automation

B   Data Processing

C   Cognitive Computing

D   Coding

173 PKL Company has decided to develop a new product and GH has been seconded to the project team for the next few months. The team is currently drawing up a series of performance measures for the development in order that they can establish whether it is successful.

Which of the following project management phases is currently underway in the project?

A   Initiation

B   Planning

C   Executing

D   Controlling

174 GHJ Company is considering investing in a new machine which will save on processing costs. However, funds are limited and the company evaluates all projects according to their payback period. The machine costs $28,000 and will save the company $5,000 immediately and then $6,000 per year for the next five years.

What is the payback period of the investment (to the nearest whole year)?

(Assume annual cash flows.)

A   1 year

B   2 years

C   4 years

D   5 years

SYLLABUS SECTION E: FINANCE INTERACTING WITH THE ORGANISATION

175 A toy retailer uses external couriers to deliver any products that are ordered online.

Which of the following KPIs is the best for measuring efficiency in the operations of the toy retailer?

A   Percentage on time delivery to customer

B   The total level of sales compared to budget

C   Percentage on time despatch of goods to customers

D   Reorder rate from customers

176 A car component manufacturing business is seeing a significant increase in components being rejected by the customer and the component returned. The business is confident in the design of the components as they have proven previously.

Which of the following techniques is best placed to help them improve their quality situation?

A   Reverse logistics

B   Kaizen

C   Measure rejection rate

D   Just-in-time

177 **In the context of just-in-time manufacturing systems, which of the following statements are true?**

(i)   It enables a more flexible offering of product to the customer

(ii)   The quality of raw materials delivered becomes more critical

A   Statement (i)

B   Statement (ii)

C   Both of them

D   Neither of them

178 The range of management issues associated with converting resources into required goods or services within an organisation is known as which of the following?

    A   Sourcing strategies

    B   Product marketing

    C   Liberalisation

    D   Operations management

179 Which of the following shows the correct sequence in the stages of product/service development?

    A   Concept screening, consider customers' needs, design process, time-to-market, product testing.

    B   Consider customers' needs, concept screening, design process, time-to-market, product testing.

    C   Consider customers' needs, concept screening, design process, product testing, time-to-market.

    D   Product testing, time-to-market, consider customers' needs, concept screening, design process.

180 Most supply chains involve which of the following?

    A   A number of different companies

    B   An organisation's infrastructure

    C   After sales service

    D   A strategic apex

181 Loss of goodwill and the expense of product recalls are known as which of the following?

    A   External failure costs

    B   Costs of lean

    C   Excess production costs

    D   Transaction costs

182 A lean approach is associated with which of the following?

    A   Supply sourcing strategies

    B   Demographic profiling

    C   Employee selection criteria

    D   Elimination of waste

183 Which of the following is not a spoke in Cousins' supply wheel?

    A   Cost benefit analysis

    B   Portfolio of relationships

    C   Performance measures

    D   A firm's infrastructure

184   **Collaborating with its suppliers may bring a company added-value because it can:**

    A   strike a harder bargain with its suppliers

    B   work with a supplier to improve quality and reduce costs

    C   avoid transaction costs

    D   introduce price competition amongst suppliers

185   The emergence of internet selling has increased the need for organisations to focus on their reverse logistics capability.

    Is this statement TRUE or FALSE?

    A   True

    B   False

186   **Which THREE of the following may be advantages of using process maps?**

    A   Highlighting opportunities to standardise processes

    B   Fewer bottlenecks to improve resource utilisation

    C   Visual representation of inefficiencies

    D   Provides an overview of responsibilities

    E   Improves relationships with suppliers

187   **Which of the following is an example of co-ordination between the finance function and procurement?**

    A   Inventory management

    B   Charge-out rates

    C   Customer service

    D   Creating purchase orders

188   **Which of the following is an example of co-ordination between the finance function and production?**

    A   Establishing credit terms

    B   Advising on prices

    C   Determining sales quantities

    D   Budgeting

189   **A computerised system for planning the requirements for raw materials, work-in-progress and finished items is known as what?**

    A   ERP

    B   MRP

    C   MRP II

    D   DSS

190 Smart turbo trainers are becoming increasingly popular. A user attaches their own bicycle to the trainer and with the help of included training software can be put through their paces to improve fitness and strength. The supplier has three versions of turbo trainer and charges three different prices for them, with the best trainer carrying the highest price. The lowest priced trainer still makes a small profit at its price. Better training software is available from third party providers at an extra cost from the third party.

Which pricing strategy is being followed by the turbo training supplier?

A   Captive product pricing

B   Loss leading

C   Perceived quality pricing

D   Price discrimination

191 In a typical modern taxi business, the fare calculation is complicated. The fare is made up of a payment for the time of the driver (this is based on statutory minimum wages plus a premium for the skill level involved), a payment for the mileage covered (this is based on 150% of the cost of fuel and other running costs of the car), an uplift percentage if demand is high or supply is low at the time of booking.

Which TWO of the following pricing strategies are incorporated here?

A   Cost-plus pricing

B   Perceived quality pricing

C   Dynamic pricing

D   Going rate pricing

192 White Knuckle Limited concentrates on providing experiences for the adventurous. It tends to separate its offerings based on water, wheels and shoes, providing different experiences in each market. All the prices set are above the norm as it provides only the best versions of each holiday type.

Which form of targeting is it using in its strategy?

A   Concentrated marketing

B   Undifferentiated marketing

C   Differentiated marketing

D   Experiential marketing

193 **Which of the following is a way in which an organisation's marketing department would co-ordinate with its finance function?**

A   Calculating charge out rates for services provided by the organisation

B   Calculating the budgets for the number of units to be produced

C   Estimation of the costs of the raw materials required for production

D   Decisions on the quality of raw materials that the organisation can afford to use

194   E Co has a large marketing department.

In which of the following ways would this department co-ordinate with E's finance function?

A   Decisions on the quantity of raw materials required

B   Establishing credit terms for customers

C   Calculating pay rises for staff

D   Decisions on the selling price of the product

195   A Ltd is considering carrying out some market research and would prefer to use field research because it tends to be quicker and cheaper than carrying out desk research.

Is this statement true or false?

A   True

B   False

196   **An organisational approach that involves targeting an entire market with a single marketing mix is known as which one of the following?**

A   Undifferentiated

B   Differentiated

C   Saturated

D   Blanket

197   **Match the forms of marketing communication in the list below to the correct definitions.**

- Viral
- Guerrilla
- Experiential
- Digital

Term	Definition
	An interactive marketing experience aimed at stimulating all the senses.
	The promotion of products or brands via one or more forms of electronic media.
	Relies on well thought out, highly focused and often unconventional attacks on key targets.
	Encourages individuals to pass on a marketing message to others, so creating exponential growth in the message's exposure.

198 Molly is currently assessing the use of intermediaries needed to get her product to the end consumers.

Which part of the marketing mix is she assessing?

A   Product

B   Price

C   Place

D   Promotion

199 **The pricing policy which involves setting a low price to gain market share is known as what?**

A   Price skimming

B   Penetration pricing

C   Price discrimination

D   Loss leaders

200 **Which TWO of the following statements are true regarding technology and market research?**

A   Organisations can conduct focus groups online through technology allowing them to interact with people across wide geographic boundaries

B   All data held online is valid

C   Due to the volume of data it now takes longer to gain business insight

D   Click analysis is a tool used to track the actions of individual users within a website

201 **Label the diagram of the product life cycle using some of the options below.**

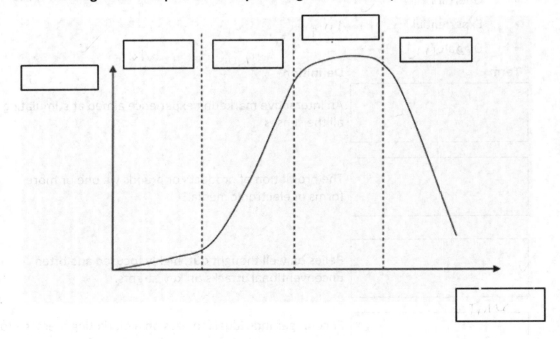

Options

- Cash
- Revenue
- Time
- Maturity
- Introduction
- Peak
- Trough
- Decline
- Growth
- Innovation

202 **Match the pricing policy to its correct description**

Pricing policy	Description
Price discrimination	Setting a high initial price when a product is new
Going rate pricing	Altering prices in line with demand
Penetration pricing	Charging a different price for the same product to a different market segment
Price skimming	Setting a low price to gain market share
Dynamic pricing	Matching competitors' prices

203 **Dividing the market into groups of homogenous people is known as what in the context of marketing?**

A   Situation analysis

B   Positioning

C   Targeting

D   Segmentation

204 Khilan is monitoring transport and storage costs as KPIs for sales and marketing.

Which element of the marketing mix is he focussing on specifically?

A   Product

B   Price

C   Place

D   Promotion

205 **Match the advantage with the performance related pay approach in the table below:**

Approach	Advantage
Individual performance related pay	Aligns the objectives of owners and managers
Group performance related pay	Information always available automatically
Profit related pay	Relates to a person's effort
Share options	Encourages togetherness

206 A human resource manager has recently organised and ran some training on the effective use of excel as a decision support system. The initial feedback was positive as were the test results from two tests held before and then after the training. All candidates showed improvement in their basic excel skills. Anecdotally and informally it appears that the excel skills are being used more in the workplace departments involved.

Which of Kirkpatrick's evaluation levels has not been proven here?

A Reaction

B Learning

C Behaviour

D Results

207 **In relation to the taking of references from an applicant's past employer, which of the following statements are true?**

(i) References should be an invaluable source of information concerning how a prospect normally behaves at work.

(ii) References can only ever be factual. When did the person start and end working, what was their position and so on? Opinions cannot be given for fear of litigation.

A Statement (i)

B Statement (ii)

C Both of them

D Neither are true

208 **Personal characteristics, qualifications and necessary experience expected of a particular post holder are normally all found in which of the following documents?**

A Job description

B Person specification

C Reference letter

D Summary appraisal meeting record

209 **Match the stage of the HR cycle below with the correct description.**

- Appraisal

- Training

- Development

- Selection

Stage	Description
	Choosing the best person for the job from a field of candidates sourced via recruitment.
	Systematic review and assessment of an employee's performance, potential and training needs.
	Formal learning to achieve the level of skills, knowledge and competence to carry out the current role.
	Realisation of a person's potential through formal and informal learning to enable them to carry out their current and future role.

210 Andrea has just attended her appraisal with her line manager. She felt that the feedback was poorly delivered and that the manager viewed it purely as a form filling exercise.

Which TWO of Lockett's barriers to effective appraisal may have been present here?

A   Chat, bureaucracy

B   Confrontation, unfinished business

C   Chat, judgement

D   Confrontation, bureaucracy

211 **An effective appraisal system involves:**

A   assessing the personality of the appraisee

B   a process initiated by the manager who needs an update from the appraisee

C   advising on the faults of the appraisee

D   a participative, problem-solving process between the manager and appraisee

212 **Which HR activity could be monitored using the KPIs of employee absenteeism and productivity?**

A   Reward systems

B   Performance management

C   Training and Development

D   Motivation

213 The psychological contract is a legally binding document that exists between an employer and an employee?

Is this statement true or false?

214 Match the type of flexible working arrangement to the correct explanation.

Type of flexible working arrangement	Explanation
Remote working/ teleworking	Working outside of normal working day patterns
Flexitime	Fewer hours than the standard weekly number
Shift system	Standard weekly hours within fewer days
Compressed week	The need to work a standard set of hours but less restriction on when these hours are worked
Job sharing	Technology has enabled employees to work away from the office, usually at home
Part-time	Two employees share a standard hour week

215 Which of the following is not an advantage of individual performance related pay?

A   Encourages teamwork

B   Employee controllability

C   Goal congruence

D   Motivation

216 Complete the following sentences from the words below.

Traditionally the HR function and the finance function worked _____.

People were regarded by finance as _____. Nowadays people are regarded as _____.

- assets
- independently
- collaboratively
- costs
- liabilities

217 **Match the HR activity to the most appropriate KPI**

Activity	KPI
Recruitment and Selection	Turnover rate
Training and Development	Competitiveness of salary
Performance management	Delegate feedback scores
Motivation	Female to male ratio
Reward system	Appraisals completed on time

218 **The "systematic review and assessment of an employee's performance, potential and training needs" describes what?**

A   Training

B   Development

C   Appraisal

D   Induction

219 Alexander is reviewing a graph which is giving him an overview of the monthly performance of his team. He notices one team member is underperforming and wishes to know more details. The system lets Alexander drill down to get further details.

What type of system is Alexander using?

A   Decision support system

B   Expert system

C   Transaction processing system

D   Executive information system

220 **What sort of system could be used to obtain specialist tax knowledge?**

A   Decision support system

B   Expert system

C   Knowledge management system

D   Executive information system

221 **What is the type of knowledge that is held by people and has not been formally documented?**

A   Explicit knowledge

B   Informal knowledge

C   Human knowledge

D   Tacit knowledge

222 Which TWO of the following are advantages of remote working for the organisation?

A   Increased control over staff

B   Reduced absenteeism

C   Reduced infrastructure costs

D   Dilution of organisation culture

223 Groupware, the intranet, and extranets are examples of what type of systems?

A   Decision support systems

B   Expert systems

C   Knowledge management systems

D   Appraisal system

224 P Co is an organisation which outsources most of its functions and exists primarily as a network of contracts.

What type of organisation is P Co?

A   Virtual organisation

B   Modular organisation

C   Matrix organisation

D   Remote organisation

225 Linda works as part of a virtual team.

Which THREE of the following challenges is she likely to face?

A   Sharing knowledge with other members of her team

B   Feelings of isolation

C   Over supervision from her line manager

D   Cultural differences

E   Lack of delegation

226 Paul has been given the task of ensuring his organisation goes beyond compliance with technology and data legislation.

What is this commitment known as?

A   Ethics

B   Corporate social responsibility

C   Corporate digital responsibility

D   Sustainability

227 **Which of the following is not a benefit of big data analytics**

A   Improved decision making

B   Market customisation

C   Increased security of data

D   Product innovation

228 **The movement of data through a process or system is also known as what?**

A   Data flow

B   Data outputs

C   Data warehousing

D   Data mining

229 Steele Co are choosing between centralised and decentralised IS architecture.

Which approach will give them greater control over their information systems?

A   Centralised

B   Decentralised

230 Raj has been analysing trends in the online reviews on social media for his organisation's main product line. However, he has noticed many inconsistencies.

Which of the 4 Vs of big data may be causing this problem?

A   Volume

B   Variety

C   Velocity

D   Veracity

231 **In the context of home working, which of the following statements are true?**

(i)   Tacit knowledge is less likely to be shared.

(ii)   In the long run, it is a cheaper way of working from both the employee and employer point of view.

A   Statement (i)

B   Statement (ii)

C   Both of them

D   Neither are true

232 Of the following controls/solutions, which provide the best protection against virus infection?

A   Strict policies on the opening of attachments

B   Segregation of duties

C   Back-up procedures

D   Time lock outs

233 Which of the following KPIs are the best indicator of good operational efficiency of an IT function?

A   IT spend per employee

B   IT utilisation rates

C   Revenue generated from new IT systems

D   Promptness of resolution

Section 2

ANSWERS TO OBJECTIVE TEST QUESTIONS

SYLLABUS SECTION A: ROLE OF THE FINANCE FUNCTION

1   A

Staffing numbers is part of resource allocation – an important role of the finance function will be working out which resources the organisation will require to achieve its objectives.

2   D

The positions of the Chairperson (person responsible for leadership and board effectiveness) and the CEO (the person in charge of running the company) should be separated to ensure that no-one person has too much power. The company does have an internal audit function to provide independent scrutiny, has a five-year plan so is not too focused on short-term profitability and has a monthly meeting with shareholders which is an excellent way of maintaining contact.

3   B, D

A remuneration committee is responsible for deciding on the pay and incentives offered to executive directors (including pension rights and compensation payments). It should be made up of only of NEDs as no director should be involved in setting the level of their own remuneration. At least three NEDs are required for FTSE 350 or larger companies and at least two for smaller listed companies. The company chairman can be a member but cannot chair the committee. The chair must have been a committee member for at least 12 months.

4

Completing work carefully, thoroughly and diligently, in accordance with relevant technical and professional standards.	Professional competence and due care
Being straightforward, honest and truthful in all professional and business relationships.	Integrity
Non-disclosure of information unless you have specific permission or a legal or professional duty to do so.	Confidentiality
Not allowing bias, conflict of interest, or the influence of other people to override your professional judgement.	Objectivity
Compliance with relevant laws and regulations.	Professional behaviour

5   C

Professional competence and due care. If Polly undertakes the work knowing that she will not be able to complete it to the best of her ability she would not be behaving with due care.

6   B

Confidentiality. Gemma must not share information unless she has specific permission or a legal duty to do so.

7   A, B, E

The reputation of a business can be enhanced if they behave in an ethical manner, this can also attract employees and new customers to increase revenue.

It may increase costs, however, this would not be a benefit.

Risk should actually reduce for a more ethical business, not increase.

8   D, E, F

Connected stakeholders have a transaction with the business, such as suppliers, customers and lenders. Employees are internal stakeholders, whilst the government and environmental pressure groups are external stakeholders.

9   A, B, D

Increased costs is an argument against the introduction of CSR principles. One of the criticisms of CSR is that businesses may just use it as a PR exercise.

10   TRUE

By definition

11   B, C, E

Increased contact with shareholders is an indication of good corporate governance.

An emphasis on short-term profitability (not long-term) would be an indicator of poor governance.

12   D

By definition

13   A

Answers B and D relate to 'enables' and answer C relates to 'narrates how'.

14   A, B, F

The nominations committee oversees appointments to the board. The remuneration committee oversees the pay of the executive directors. The audit committee acts as a liaison between the directors and the auditors.

15   D

The positions of the Chairman (the person who runs the board) and the CEO (the person in charge of running the company) should be separated. This is to ensure that no one individual has too much power within the company.

16   B

To be considered as an independent NED, an individual must not have been an employee of the company in the last five years.

17   D

The nominations committee ensures that all appointments are based on merit and suitability and that the composition of the board is balanced.

18   C

Traditionalists do not believe in corporate social responsibility (CSR) and have the opinion that a business should not exceed its obligations for stakeholders.

19   A

Internal stakeholders are those within the business, for example employees.

Connected stakeholders are those who have a transaction with the business, for example customers and suppliers.

External stakeholders are those outside of the business, for example the general public.

20

Stakeholder	Need/expectation
Employees	Pay, working conditions and job security
Shareholders	Dividends and capital growth
Government	Provision of taxes and jobs and compliance with legislation
Customers	Value-for-money products and services

21 D

The person in charge of running the company is the chief executive officer not the chairman. The chairman is the person in charge of running the board.

22

The preparation of forecasts, for example of future sales or material prices, will be an important role of the finance function in enabling the organisation to create and preserve value.

The preparation of comprehensive reports for shareholders will be an important role of the finance function in narrating how the organisation creates and preserves value.

The preparation of variance analysis for control purposes will be an important role of the finance function in shaping how the organisation creates and preserves value.

23 A

Schools is the correct answer because the other organisations are normally found in the private (i.e. non-governmental) sector.

24 D

Both these statements are false. The 'narrates how' role involves financial (corporate) reporting, the 'shapes how' role includes performance management and control.

The finance function should attempt to anticipate potential changes and be ready to respond.

25 C

The sacking of someone for gross misconduct is not in itself poor CSR, the employee may well have deserved the treatment. Products often have known failure rates (light bulbs) and as long as false claims are not made this is not necessarily poor CSR. Redundancy is sometimes necessary to save the company and the jobs of the majority.

26 C

All the examples contain an agency relationship of some sort, but C is the generally accepted definition of agency risk.

27 FALSE

Not-for-profit organisations will also be affected by rapid changes in technology. The finance function will need to adapt in these types of entities just as much as within profit seeking entities.

28 C and D are true

Whilst change may bring about risk (A) is can also present opportunities.

Despite change being unpredictable (B), organisations still have to plan for different ways of doing business.

All businesses will be affected in some way, even the smallest businesses.

29 C

The information is taking 14 hours to gather which will cost money. If it is immediately being filed, the benefit will be less than this cost.

30 E

The fifth A is Analyse not Align.

31 C

Assembling information involves collecting data from a range of sources.

32 TRUE

By definition

33 B

Analyse for insights could take the form of comparing actual to budget. This activity can also be viewed as the broad role of questioning.

34 A, B and D

The data can have relevance to the organisation (answer C) although it may not meet the exact needs of the business.

It is not unethical to use external data as long as the data has been gathered in an ethical manner.

35 B

By definition

36 A, B and E

These are all examples of internal sources of data. Newspaper articles and exchange rate information would be gathered from external sources.

37 D

This can be seen on the below diagram.

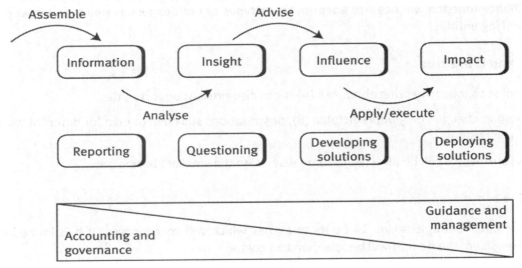

38 A

Information which contains typos or casting errors is not accurate.

39 B

Providing insight to users by analysing information can take the form of a comparison of the information with the budgeted or historical figures.

40 C

Sales growth of 20% may not be significant if it is put into context, for example if the industry is growing by 35% (answer A).

Non-financial data can sometimes be quantified, it can still be expressed in numerical terms, for example number of complaints (answer B).

Good quality analysis does rely on a representative sample of the population (answer C).

Number of training days is non-financial, not non-quantifiable. It can be counted (answer D).

41 D

Finance professionals apply the information to harness value for the organisation through their impact. This activity can also be viewed as the broad role of deploying solutions.

42 B, E, F

Quantitative measures are numerical, whereas, qualitative performance measure are non-numerical. Sales, profit and number of units produced are all numerical measures of performance.

43   A

Reporting on current pricing structures is providing Information, as is monitoring compliance with regulations. Forecasting sales figures is providing Insights. Setting prices is the implementation of a decision to achieve the desired goal which is known as Impact or Execute.

44   A

Acumen is the process of connecting different activities to each other. Finance professionals can prepare valuable information on the outcomes achieved from various initiatives in order to inform future proposals.

SYLLABUS SECTION B: TECHNOLOGY IN A DIGITAL WORLD

45   B

By definition

46   D

By definition

47   A

This describes the basic idea of cloud computing.

48   A and C

Public clouds are hosted by 3rd parties. Private clouds are managed over a private infrastructure.

49   B, C and D

The contract with the cloud provider will require careful management, this also increases reliance on the 3rd party and can result in job losses in IT support and maintenance roles.

Scalability, increased flexibility and reduced cost are all advantages of cloud computing.

50   B, C and E

Option A is incorrect in that big data does not refer to any specific financial amount. Option D is also incorrect. Big data can indeed come from many sources, but this is too narrow a definition. Big data refers to the large volume of data, the many sources of data and the many types of data.

51

    A   National Statistics – **Open**

    B   Social media posts – **Human Sourced**

    C   Emails – **Human Sourced**

    D   Smart meters – **Machine Generated**

    E   Customer database – **Processed**

    F   Census – **Open**

    G   Home assistants – **Machine Generated**

    H   Fixed asset register – **Processed**

52 C

Increasingly process automation is focussing on more complex business areas which can save costs and enable employees to focus on more value adding activities.

53 C

This is a description of artificial intelligence.

54 B

By definition

55 A, B and D

In order to increase security and address the issue of cyber risk, all of the transactions in a blockchain are publically available and all transactions must be verified by a decentralised network of computers.

56 D

By definition. Answer C is too narrow an explanation although is an example of the use of the internet of things. Answer B is the definition of blockchain.

57 TRUE

News is now consumed via mobile devices and is live rather than being a record of yesterday's news.

58 B

By definition

59 C

This best describes the process of 3-D printing.

60   A, C and D

Traditional industries such as banking and the news have now been replaced by online versions and apps. Music is also now being downloaded or streamed instantly.

Social media interactions (B) have increased, and the costs have declined for manufacturers as the technologies develop (E).

61   B, D and E

A is incorrect as 3-D printing does not involve batch production (traditional manufacture which is more focused on large volumes of identical products).

C is incorrect as there are no off-cuts with 3-D printing. 3-D printing sees the exact design printed and nothing else.

62   A, B and C

Cloud technology allows pay as you go computing charged based on what a company actually needs and is therefore cost efficient.

Cloud computing allows frequent upgrades making it scalable.

Cloud computing supports remote working increasing flexibility.

63   D

By definition. Veracity considers the reliability of the data being received.

64   A

The most common use of data visualisation is in creating a dashboard to display the key performance indicators of a business in a live format, thus allowing immediate understanding of current performance.

B is incorrect as the data is displayed in customisable formats.

Data visualisation has nothing to do with virtual reality (answer C).

D is incorrect as a core element of data visualisation is understanding and ease of use, hence removing the need for IT professionals.

65   B

Data analytics can help an organisation analyse its customers into specific segments and understand more about their wants and needs. Process automation is the use of technology to perform complex business processes. Artificial intelligence is where a machine can interpret and learn from external data such as voice recognition. Data visualisation is the displaying of complex data in a visually appealing and accessible way.

66   B, C, D

The internet of things describes the network of smart devices with inbuilt software and connectivity to the internet allowing them to constantly monitor and exchange data. This would include responding to remote instructions, tracking external temperatures and remitting information back to GHP. Controlling and adjusting the internal temperature of the warehouse is a standard requirement of any closed loop system and does not require access to the internet.

67   A

These technologies which are considered to be main stream are termed core modernisation tools, examples include the cloud.

68   B

These technologies are still at the early adopter stage and are termed exponentials, examples include blockchain.

69   B

Many cloud services are provided by external third parties, and therefore reliance on these suppliers will be increased.

70   FALSE

Multiple users can collaborate at the same time but cloud computing reduces the risk of version control issues.

71   A, D and E

Training (answer B) will still be required for staff to understand how the new software works and interfaces with their roles.

Process automation changes the way the finance function works and can lead to uncertainty around job security and future prospects, there will not necessarily be automatic buy in by the staff (answer C).

72   D

By definition

73   A

The graphic produced will only be as accurate as the original data. Visualisation does not improve this accuracy.

74   B

Statements (i) and (iii) are true.

Statement (ii) is false because there is no agreement yet as to how these assets should be accounted for.

Statement (iv) is incorrect as cross border payments should be made much simpler through the use of blockchain.

75   A

The impact of 3-D printing on the finance function is largely from a costing perspective, practically dealing with the changes in operations this technology allows.

76   A, C and D

The remaining two qualities are 'give up control yet architect the choices' and 'rely on data yet trust your intuition'.

77   B

The intangible assets of the company such as a network of contacts are internally generated and therefore cannot be recognised on the statement of financial position, this may understate their true value.

78   B

The new technology is driving an expansion beyond sample-based testing to include analysis of entire populations of audit-relevant data, using intelligent analytics to deliver a higher quality of audit evidence and more relevant business insights.

Whilst statement D is correct, it has more relevance to the management accounting function than internal audit.

Statements A and C are false.

79   FALSE

Accounting for cryptocurrency is currently a grey area for standard setters and exactly how they should be classified is subject to ongoing debate.

80   D

Use of mobile technology has reduced duplication and data entry. App software for logging and recording expenses has reduced manual processing, whilst delivering significant efficiencies and better quality management information.

81   C

Judgement involves making decisions, evaluating data sources and applying knowledge to make sound judgements.

82   A

This describes business acumen.

83   B, C and D

GDPR requires data to be kept for no longer than is necessary, it does not suggest a number of years (answer A). Data can be stored in a variety of formats and therefore answer E is incorrect.

84   FALSE

Compliance with legislation such as the GDPR laws is something that all companies should achieve. However, there are also ethical considerations as to what companies do and how they act.

85   A and C

CDR goes beyond mere compliance and is a voluntary commitment which will improve the risk management of the business.

86   C

Digital inclusion is about ensuring all members of society have the skills, tools and ability to access the online digital world, and are not left behind through lack of education or opportunity. Businesses need to be proactive to help and support users and reduce barriers and obstacles. Answer A focuses on 'data value', answer B focuses on 'customer expectations' and answer D focuses on 'giving back'.

87   C

Digital inclusion is about ensuring all members of society have the skills, tools and ability to access the online digital world, and are not left behind through lack of education or opportunity. Businesses need to be proactive to help and support users and reduce barriers and obstacles.

88   A, D, E

A digital mindset is about seeing beyond the individual elements of digital change, to understand the deeper ways in which digital technology will ultimately transform every aspect of society and therefore impact an organisation. Management must maintain a clear vision whilst empowering employees to make the changes needed to adapt. They should sustain existing business practices and be sceptical (though open-minded) about the new technologies available. They should trust their intuition and use the data as a basis for developing their vision.

SYLLABUS SECTION C: DATA AND INFORMATION IN A DIGITAL WORLD

89

Jane – operational

Bill – strategic

Colleen – tactical

90 FALSE

Whilst the statement about enhancing competitive advantage is true, valuable information can also offer significant cost savings through improvements to operational efficiencies.

91 A, B and E

C and D are ways that data and technology can support the operations function, rather than marketing.

92 A, B and C

D is how data and technology can support the HR function.

E is how data and technology can support the marketing function.

93 D

Digital assets are assets held by a business in digital form that do not have physical substance.

94 B

The videos would be an example of a digital asset.

95 C and D

The access is both in a single central location and only allowed with the correct authorisation, making A and B incorrect.

96 FALSE

Version control, watermarking and embargo dates allow increased security and protect assets from improper use. Additionally, access levels built into the system allow access only to those with authorisation.

97 D

Tactical decisions are medium term and involve putting the strategic plan into action.

98   C

A digital asset management system is designed to coordinate the digital assets of a business, ensuring they are held centrally in an accessible, secure and logically designed repository.

99   C

The three decision making systems support each other. Operational errors might well cause cost overruns.

100   B

The sales invoice total is data only. The lead time information is not relevant to the sales director and the price list is again just data without analysis.

101   D

By definition.

102   B

Admittedly the technology makes data gathering more efficient and quicker but the nature of the data is also changing, with more information than was previously available being gathered. For example, a customer may have considered an alternative before buying, in the past this fact would be lost. Short lead times enable business to respond to the signals and trend that data is revealing.

103   D

Permission cannot be shared and increasingly digital assets are protected. Embargo dates can be used to withdraw permissions after a certain time.

104   D

By definition

Answers A and C are strategic decisions whilst B describes operational decision making.

105   A

Decisions about mergers and acquisitions happen at the strategic level.

106   D

Data can enable new market segments to be identified, which may previously have been lost within a broader market segment.

107   D

Data from past product launches and company promotions for an entire industry combined with the subsequent sales performance of those products provides huge insight into what promotions work best and when. This can reduce the guesswork by supporting companies with real data.

108   B

Deviations from expected performance give early warning of potential problems and preventative maintenance can be scheduled at a convenient time and before an asset breaks down.

109   D

Storage of data is covered by the legislation, since access is an important security issue. Each business must assess what information they need and for what purpose, this is likely to be different for different types of businesses. A bank for example is not the same as a milkman in terms of the information it needs.

110   A

The sales function would require live data on competitors' pricing and market trends to enable them to set selling prices.

111   C

The HR function requires data to incorporate appraisal systems, productivity analysis as well as collecting data on internal progressions and training days.

112   B

Sales will, for example, require live data on competitors' pricing and market trends and will require metrics on key customer feedback about products and services.

113   B

The directors seek insight and clarity form information provided by finance, this is often required in the form of data visualisation. However, all stakeholders may use data visualisation, just for different reasons.

114   C

Extraction, transformation, loading

115

Level	Description
Conceptual	Business oriented and practical, considering the business data and its requirements
Logical	This level begins to develop a technical map of rules and data structures defining how data will be held and used
Physical	This considers how the defined system requirements will be implemented using a specific database management system

116 B

By definition

117 B

By definition

118 D

The constant stream of data being produced in real time, is referred to as the velocity of big data.

119 A

This describes business intelligence.

120 D

ETL stands for extraction, transformation and loading. The ETL system is a single tool combining the processes of extraction (answer A), transformation (answer B) and loading (answer C).

121 A

Data visualisation is an enabling technology that complements data analytics by facilitating user friendly and accessible presentation of key data.

122 B

Veracity relates to the extent that the data can be relied upon. Systems must ensure data can be validated to reduce uncertainty to tolerable levels.

123 D

Finance professionals will need people skills; building empathy and interactions with stakeholders. Technical skills include the application of accounting and finance skills and leadership skills focus on areas such as team building and the ability to motivate and inspire. Finance professionals will also require business skills and digital skills but will usually work with data scientists rather than requiring data scientist skills.

124 D

Whilst the directors will be looking at this data, they're doing so wondering what a lender will make of the figures. Shareholders might also be interested but again it is the lenders that are more concerned about these metrics.

125 D

Too much data is possible. It could be too expensive to calculate, too detailed or overly confusing. An average, whilst potentially useful, is unlikely to be enough to manage the business.

126   C

By definition

The data strategy should establish clear, consistent user friendly policies on the use and storage of data to ensure correct use and minimise risk of data breaches.

127   B

Structural is not a level in a data modelling process. The three levels of a data modelling process are conceptual, logical and physical.

128   D

The order is wrong in both these statements. Data is profiled, then extracted, transformed and loaded in to a data warehouse.

129   B, C and E

The detail described in answer A is too detailed for the infographic. Access will not necessarily be suitable for all sales staff as described in answer D.

130   B

There are many new possibilities for data analysis since there is also a change in the nature of the data. Statistical significance testing, for example, may become a required skill. Experts (data scientists) are becoming more common as a support to accountants.

SYLLABUS SECTION D: SHAPE AND STRUCTURE OF THE FINANCE FUNCTION

131   C

The company has identified the skills its staff will need in order to carry out their work and requires them to all have a standard qualification. This standardisation of skills is common in a professional bureaucracy such as an architects practice, a hospital or a law firm.

(Note: Co-ordinating mechanisms are discussed in an expandable text in the Study Text on Mintzberg's effective organisation and knowledge of this is not required for the exam. However, you should be able to answer this question by using the information given in the scenario).

132   A, C, E

Increasing the levels of management (i.e. creating a longer scalar chain) leads to a tall organisation with narrow spans of control (the number of staff reporting to each manager). However, it is likely to have higher levels of bureaucracy so that decisions take longer to be made.

133   B

Because the entrepreneurial structure is run by one person who makes all the decisions, this powerful individual will have strong control over the organisation and its strategic direction, leading to better goal congruence.

134   D

Function managers may make decisions to increase their own power, or in the interests of their own function, rather than in the interests of the company overall. Economies of scale, standardisation and specialists feeling comfortable are advantages of a functional structure.

135   D

A refers to an entrepreneurial structure.

B is typical of a functional structure.

C describes a divisional structure.

In a matrix structure individuals will have dual command, a functional manager and a divisional manager. This can cause conflict between departments and stress for the individual.

136   C and D

The first two features relate to a functional structure.

137   A

If H wants to manage each product separately, it will need to adopt either a matrix or divisional approach, as these would allow the creation of separate divisions for each product. However, H wishes to keep its administrative costs as low as possible. As the matrix structure has high admin costs due to high numbers of managers, A should adopt a divisional approach.

138   D

The granting of authority over each divisional geographic area to geographic bosses results in a potential loss of control over key operating decisions. This weakness is also present in the product divisional structure.

139   A

The span of control is the number of people for whom a manager is directly responsible.

Scalar chain relates to the number of management levels within an organisation.

140

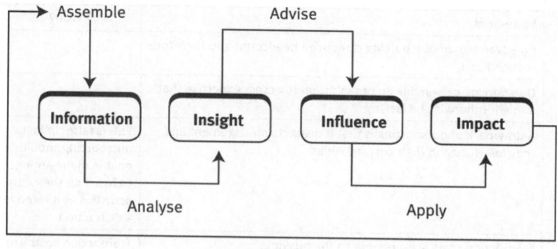

141 A

Assembling information can be viewed as the broad role of reporting where there is an emphasis on accounting and governance (for example, financial reporting, management accounting, regulatory compliance, risk management and corporate governance).

142 **Technology and automation** will play an important role in all of the activities of the finance function but will have the largest impact on the '**assembly**' and '**analysis**' activities.

This will 'free up' the resource of the finance function professionals who can now place greater focus on the '**advising**' and '**applying/executing**' activities.

143

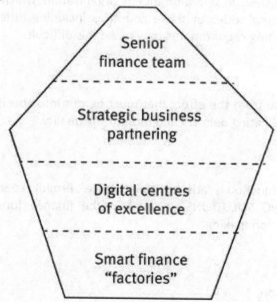

144

Statement	True?
An advantage of outsourcing is reduced headcount and therefore reduced cost	✓
Outsourcing can enable an organisation to access expertise that it might otherwise be lacking	✓
A drawback of outsourcing is that it distracts management and they lose focus on their core activities	This is false. In fact, outsourcing should enable management to focus on their core activities as it removes a distraction
Transaction costs are a benefit to the business	Transaction costs are an expense not a benefit
Outsourcing may lead to redundancies which can affect employee morale	✓

145 A, B, D

Shared service centres provide the opportunity to standardise processes and to consolidate systems, which makes control easier and allows for consistent reporting.

Empire building is a disadvantage of a functional structure.

Advancements in technology are not a benefit of shared service centres but rather has facilitated their development.

A shared service centre is often established in a multinational organisation which has operations in several countries. The complexities of these countries including different laws, taxes, languages, cultures and reporting requirements may make this difficult.

146 A

When outsourcing, transaction costs arise from the effort that must be put into specifying what is required and subsequently co-ordinating delivery and monitoring quality.

147

One of the main activities of the finance function is 'advising to influence'. Broadly speaking this can be referred to as DEVELOPING SOLUTIONS. It involves the finance function communicating insights to influence decision making.

148 RPA

RPA stands for Robotic Process Automation

BPR stands for Business Process Re-engineering, TQM means Total Quality Management, and Kaizen is a philosophy of continual improvement.

149 C

The strategic level of the finance function is more likely to focus on information for external stakeholders.

150 A

The treasury department will monitor foreign exchange and try to minimise the company's exposure to foreign exchange losses.

151 D

The other three are correct for financial accounting.

152 (i)   B

(ii)   B

(iii)   A

(iv)   A

153 B

EPS measures the profit attributable to each ordinary shareholder.   The P/E ratio measures the share price divided by the EPS.

154 B

While treasurers will deal with cash management (amongst other things) they do not produce cash flow statements – this is part of the role of a financial accounting function. C and D would both be undertaken by a management accountant.

155 C

A, B and D are not true. They describe advantages of using the issue of share capital to finance investment.

156 A

Debt tends to be cheaper to service than equity. However, a company cannot normally suspend debt repayments if it can no longer afford them – this is only possible with dividends. Dividends are not an allowable deduction, but interest is. Finally, shareholders would not normally receive any security on their investment, meaning that D is also incorrect.

157 A

This is tax evasion as the company is illegally reducing its tax liability. Note that it cannot be both evasion and avoidance simultaneously.

158 D

Tax mitigation involves conduct that reduces the organisation's tax liability without defeating the intentions of the law makers. It would there for be classed as legal.

Tax avoidance is used to describe schemes which, whilst they are legal, are designed to defeat the intentions of the law makers. Thus, once a tax avoidance scheme becomes public knowledge, the law makers will usually step in to change the law to stop the scheme from working.

159 B, C, G and H

These statements all relate to internal audit. The other statements (A, D, E and F) relate to external audit.

160 B

The internal audit also makes recommendations for the achievement of company objectives. C is the role of the external auditors.

161 A

Financial Planning and Analysis (FP&A) specialists play a crucial role in organisations by performing budgeting, forecasting and data analysis that supports the major organisational decisions of the board.

162 D

Project appraisal involves an assessment and appraisal of the many decisions and potential outcomes of a particular project.

163 C

Project management is the integration of all aspects of a project, ensuring that the proper knowledge and resources are available when and where needed, and above all to ensure the expected outcome is produced in a timely, cost effective manner.

164 D

Project appraisal will take place as part of the first stage (initiation) of project management. One of the most important decisions that will need to be appraised is the capital investment decision.

165 A – FALSE. The finance function works alongside these specialists providing expert support for decisions and projects and helps to formulate strategies so that the business is able to adapt to the ever changing environment.

B – FALSE. This is the responsibility of Financial Planning and Analysis.

C – TRUE. All projects are different and it is the role of the project management to integrate all aspects of it.

D – TRUE. Today is known as time 0 in project appraisal.

166   A, C and D are the correct answers

B is incorrect because although technology improves the productivity of the finance function, it is still a vital function within an organisation.

E is incorrect because the digital centres of excellence provide further insight into value creation. They are not performing routine tasks.

167   Level two of the diamond shaped finance function involves **communicating** insight to **influence** users. This must be delivered in an appropriate **format**, and with appropriate **frequency**.

168   C

Strategic business partnering sees the finance function acting as a business partner **influencing** the organisation's decisions to achieve the desired organisational **impact**.

169

Statement	True/False?
The CEO is the leader of the finance team.	False, the leader of the finance team is the CFO (Chief Financial Officer).
The leader of the finance team is responsible for executing and funding strategies.	True, it is their responsibility to lead the finance team to achieve the desired organisational impact including the executing and funding of strategies set out by the CEO.
The CFO needs a skill set outside of the traditional finance skills.	True, the CFO requires skills such as regulation, risk management, business transformation, supply chain management and IT.
Technology has had minimal impact on the leader of the finance function as he/she is so senior in the organisation.	False, the CFO is increasingly relying on automation of key business processes and is relying more on technology to transform data into actionable insights that can influence and impact the organisation's achievement of its goals.

170   A, C

Technology and automation will play an important role in all of the activities of the finance function but will have the largest impact on the 'assembly' and 'analysis' activities.

171

172 C

The term cognitive computing has been used to refer to new hardware and/or software that mimics the functioning of the human brain.

173 C

Planning involves drawing up detailed plans such as communicating what has to be done, when and by whom, identifying the resources needed and establishing measures of success for the project.

174 C

The payback period is calculated as:

Year	Cash flow	Cumulative cash flow
0	-28,000 + 5,000	-23000
1	6000	-17000
2	6000	-11000
3	6000	-5000
4	6000	1000
5	6000	7000

The project therefore pays back at the end of the fourth year.

SYLLABUS SECTION E: FINANCE INTERACTING WITH THE ORGANISATION

175 C

All the business can do is despatch on time once an order is made. Delivery itself is outside its control (answer A). Sales can go up for many reasons other than efficiency of operations (lower prices, for example)(answer B). Equally, a customer may well order again and that could be a reflection of efficiency, but it could be a reflection of other factors such as cheap pricing for example (answer D).

176 B

Kaizen is a bottom up, shop floor-based philosophy designed to allow the operational staff suggest process improvements. If the design of the components is good, then the problem could be in the shop floor manufacturing processes.

Reverse logistics (answer A) improvements will merely get the components back efficiently and measuring rejection rate (answer B) will not improve the situation. Just-in-time systems (answer D) seem largely irrelevant here.

177 C

Given the product offered to the customer will have yet been made then in theory the customer can ask for a wider variety of product features. Given materials arrive "just-in-time" for current production then when they do arrive they must be perfect as any rejection will lead to delays.

178 D

By definition

179 B

The correct sequence in the stages of product/ service development is consider customers' needs, concept screening, design process, time-to-market, product testing.

180 A

Most companies outsource at least part of their supply chain.

181 A

By definition

182 D

Lean management is a philosophy that aims to systematically eliminate waste.

183 D

Cousins' strategic supply wheel is made up of five spokes; organisation structure, relationships with suppliers, cost/benefit, competences and performance measures.

184 B

It is now recognised that successful management of suppliers is based upon collaboration. A company should be able to improve quality and reduce costs as a result of this collaboration.

185 A – TRUE

Internet selling has increased the average level of returns received by an organisation and has resulted in an increased focus on their reverse logistics capability in order to reduce costs, improve customer service and increase revenue.

186 A, C and D

B and E are benefits of improved supply chain management.

187 A

Purchasing will consult with the inventory section of the finance function to determine the quantity of items already in stock and therefore the quantity required.

188 D

Production will decide how many items of what type are to be produced. The cost of producing these will be determined by the finance function and production together, and incorporated into the overall budget.

189 B

Material Requirement Planning (MRP). This system is designed to answer what is needed, how much is needed and when is it needed.

190 C

The better trainers carry the highest prices and the poorest trainers the lowest prices. This is perceived quality pricing.

The software provided works and a user does not have to buy the better version, so this is not captive product pricing (answer A). All products make a profit and so there is no evidence of loss leading (answer B). In price discrimination (answer D), the same product is sold at different prices to different customers. There is no evidence of this.

191 A, C

The fuel and the labour are both cost plus, and the uplift is dynamic. There is no evidence for either perceived quality pricing (answer B) or going rate-based pricing (answer D).

192   C

White Knuckle has clearly targeted three segments of the holiday market and has developed products for each segment.   This is differentiated marketing, rather than concentrated marketing (answer A) or undifferentiated marketing (answer B).   Experiential marketing (answer D) is technically not a form of targeting.

193   A

Option A would most likely be a marketing or service provision crossover with the finance function.   The other options relate to co-ordination between the production department and the finance function.

194   D

The finance function can help ensure a profitable selling price is used for E's products.

195   B

Secondary (desk) research is data that is already available and is therefore quicker and cheaper than carrying out primary research.   Primary research (field) research involves the collection of new information directly from respondents and therefore tends to be more expensive and slower than secondary (desk) research.

196   A

By definition

197

Term	Definition
Viral	Encourages individuals to pass on a marketing message to others, so creating exponential growth in the message's exposure.
Guerrilla	Relies on well thought out, highly focused and often unconventional attacks on key targets.
Experiential	An interactive marketing experience aimed at stimulating all the senses.
Digital	The promotion of products or brands via one or more forms of electronic media.

198   C

Place within the marketing mix includes the use of intermediaries, as well as distribution channels, transportation and storage.

199   B

By definition

200 A and D

B is not correct, just because the data is held online does not automatically mean that it is valid.

C is not correct, business insight can be gained faster and more comprehensively than before.

201

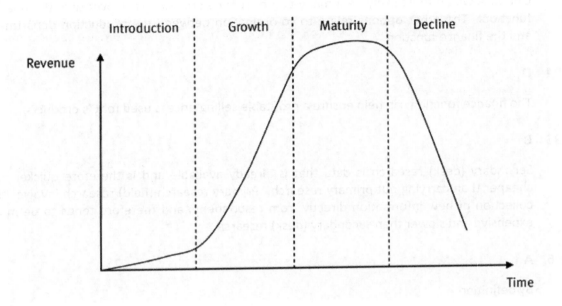

202

Pricing policy	Description
Price discrimination	Charging a different price for the same product to a different market segment
Going rate pricing	Matching competitors' prices
Penetration pricing	Setting a low price to gain market share
Price skimming	Setting a high initial price when a product is new
Dynamic pricing	Altering prices in line with demand

203 D

Market segmentation is the process of sub-dividing the market into homogenous groups to whom a separate marketing mix can be focused.

204 C

Place includes distribution of the product which also includes transportation and storage.

205

Approach	Advantage
Individual performance related pay	Relates to a person's effort
Group performance related pay	Encourages togetherness
Profit related pay	Information always available automatically
Share options	Aligns the objectives of owners and managers

206 D

The most difficult thing to prove regarding the effectiveness of training is whether it has made a difference to the business itself. Did the decision making improve? Measurement of, or assessing of the results (answer D) has not been done here.

Reaction (feedback), learning (the tests) and behaviour (observation and anecdotal evidence) are all covered.

207 A

Whilst a contentious area a reference **should** be useful and **should** give an insight as described. References do not **have** to be factual, although many firms have chosen to go that way. The grammar in this item is central.

208 B

By definition

209

Stage	Description
Selection	Choosing the best person for the job from a field of candidates sourced via recruitment.
Appraisal	Systematic review and assessment of an employee's performance, potential and training needs.
Training	Formal learning to achieve the level of skills, knowledge and competence to carry out the current role.
Development	Realisation of a person's potential through formal and informal learning to enable them to carry out their current and future role.

210 D

Feedback being poorly delivered is an example of confrontation. The manager viewing appraisal as purely a form filling exercise is an example of bureaucracy.

211 D

A key word in the question is 'effective'. Effective appraisal requires a dialogue between the manager and the person being appraised (the 'appraisee'). Any problems with the appraisee's work or performance are identified and should be discussed and resolved constructively. Answer C, in contrast, describes an ineffective appraisal process.

212 D

Low rates of employee absenteeism and high productivity can indicate a high level of motivation of the workforce.

213 FALSE

Unlike the employment contract, the psychological contract is highly subjective, not written down and not legally binding.

214

Type of flexible working arrangement	Explanation
Remote working/ teleworking	Technology has enabled employees to work away from the office, usually at home
Flexitime	The need to work a standard set of hours but less restriction on when these hours are worked
Shift system	Working outside of normal working day patterns
Compressed week	Standard weekly hours within fewer days
Job sharing	Two employees share a standard hour week
Part-time	Fewer hours than the standard weekly number

215 A

Individual performance related pay can sometimes result in a lack of team work as individuals may pursue their own goals at the expense of others.

216

Traditionally the HR function and the finance function worked **independently**.

People were regarded by finance as **costs**. Nowadays people are regarded as **assets**.

217

Activity	KPI
Recruitment and Selection	Female to male ratio
Training and Development	Delegate feedback scores
Performance management	Appraisals completed on time
Motivation	Turnover rate
Reward system	Competitiveness of salary

218 C

By definition

219 D

An executive information system (EIS) gives senior management access to internal and external information. Information is presented in a flexible, user-friendly, summarised form with the option to 'drill down' to a greater level of detail.

220 B

Expert systems hold specialist knowledge to allow non-experts to interrogate them for information.

221 D

Tacit knowledge is personal knowledge and expertise held by people within the organisation that has not been formally documented, for example knowledge gained through the experiences of employees within the organisation.

222 B, C

Control over staff will be reduced but lower infrastructure costs and reduced absenteeism are possible advantages. Dilution of organisational culture is a disadvantage.

223 C

These are examples of technology that can assist in knowledge management.

224 A

A virtual organisation is one which outsources most or all of its functions to other organisations and simply exists as a network of contracts, with very few, if any, functions being kept in-house.

225 A, B and D

Knowledge sharing may prove more difficult due to the absence of face to face contact.

Some team members may find this way of working isolating.

Team members will be from different backgrounds and cultural differences may make working together more difficult.

226 C

Corporate Digital Responsibility (CDR) is a voluntary commitment by organisations to go beyond mere compliance with legislation, when it comes to how they handle technology and data.

227 C

The security of data is a major concern in the majority of organisations and if the organisation lacks the resources to manage data then there is likely to be a greater risk of leaks and losses.

228 A

Data flow is the movement of data through a process or system. It includes data inputs, data processing and data outputs.

229 A

Centralisation often leads to greater control at a central level, enabling greater goal congruence.

230 D

Veracity refers to the reliability of the data being analysed. Often online reviews are difficult to rely upon.

231 C

Tacit knowledge is knowledge known only to the employees. If employees are working remotely then it is less likely to be shared via casual conversations. The employee saves travel costs and the employer, in the long-run, will save infrastructure costs. There may of course be some initial set up costs but in most cases the long run savings are greater.

232 A

The most common loophole into a system is personnel opening attachments that they shouldn't. Back-ups (answer C) help recover the position but not the initial infection. Time lock outs (answer D) prevent some unauthorised access to machines, but most infections originate from people outside the organisation. Segregation of duties (answer B), whilst a sensible control does not prevent virus infections.

233 D

Speedy resolution of IT problems reflect IT function efficiency. IT spend per employee (answer A) is an economic issue, IT utilisation (answer B) is an effectiveness issue as is revenue generation (answer C).